WEIPPE PUBLIC LIBRARY
P. O. Box 435
105 N. 1st Street E.
Weippe, Idaho 83553

THE  *Allure*

OF HOPE

GOD'S PURSUIT OF A
WOMAN'S HEART

JAN MEYERS

FOREWORD BY JOHN ELDREDGE

NAVPRESS

BRINGING TRUTH TO LIFE
P.O. Box 35001, Colorado Springs, Colorado 80935

3 1853 01299 0557

OUR GUARANTEE TO YOU

We believe so strongly in the message of our books that we are making this quality guarantee to you. If for any reason you are disappointed with the content of this book, return the title page to us with your name and address and we will refund to you the list price of the book. To help us serve you better, please briefly describe why you were disappointed. Mail your refund request to: NavPress, P.O. Box 35002, Colorado Springs, CO 80935.

The Navigators is an international Christian organization. Our mission is to reach, disciple, and equip people to know Christ and to make Him known through successive generations. We envision multitudes of diverse people in the United States and every other nation who have a passionate love for Christ, live a lifestyle of sharing Christ's love, and multiply spiritual laborers among those without Christ.

NavPress is the publishing ministry of The Navigators. NavPress publications help believers learn biblical truth and apply what they learn to their lives and ministries. Our mission is to stimulate spiritual formation among our readers.

© 2001 by Jan Meyers
All rights reserved. No part of this publication may be reproduced in any form without written permission from NavPress, P.O. Box 35001, Colorado Springs, CO 80935.
www.navpress.com
Library of Congress Catalog-in-Publication Number: 00-053692
ISBN 1-57683-263-5

Parts of chapter nine of the present work appeared in a somewhat different version in Jan Meyers, "Compassion—The Memory of Splendor: Grieving the Absence of Christ in Our Lives," *Mars Hill Review* 7 (winter/spring 1997): 9-20. Reprinted with permission.

Cover design by Jennifer Mahalik
Cover photo by The Image Bank
Creative Team: Eric Stanford, Lori Mitchell, Glynese Northam

Some of the anecdotal illustrations in this book are true to life and are included with the permission of the persons involved. All other illustrations are composites of real situations, and any resemblance to people living or dead is coincidental.

Unless otherwise identified, all Scripture quotations in this publication are taken from the Holy Bible, New Living Translation (NLT), copyright © 1996. Used by permission of Tyndale House Publishers, Inc., Wheaton, Illinois 60189. All rights reserved. Other versions used include: the New American Standard Bible (NASB), © The Lockman Foundation 1960, 1962, 1963, 1968, 1971, 1972, 1973, 1975, 1977; the HOLY BIBLE: NEW INTERNATIONAL VERSION® (NIV®), copyright © 1973, 1978, 1984 by International Bible Society, used by permission of Zondervan Publishing House, all rights reserved; and the King James Version (KJV).

Printed in the United States of America

2 3 4 5 6 7 8 9 10 / 05 04 03 02 01

FOR A FREE CATALOG OF
NAVPRESS BOOKS & BIBLE STUDIES,
CALL 1-800-366-7788 (USA)
OR 1-416-499-4615 (CANADA)

Another one for you, Brent

Contents

She was the most refreshing picture of femininity I have seen in a long, long time . . . and I almost missed her entirely. It happened while I was waiting to board a flight on the West Coast, one of many passengers jostling for position, eager to get down the jetway and find our seats. Normally I'm lost in thought during this too-familiar routine, running on autopilot, simply wanting to get home. But this lovely little girl caught my eye, and I found myself holding off for a moment to watch her. She was seven, I guessed, with green eyes and brown hair pulled back with a pair of those simple barrettes schoolgirls often use. She wore a denim jumper and white tennis shoes—clearly a new outfit for a special trip. But what made her so very lovely were her tears.

Her beleaguered mother was busy trying to herd a younger brother and sister and their carry-on baggage down to the plane, but this little brown-haired girl just let the crowd push by, as I did, and stood there crying. I noticed that her father remained at the top of the ramp. Apparently, he was seeing them all off on a trip to Grandmother's but promised to join them shortly. "I'll see you on Tuesday," he said with reassurance. "I love you, Daddy," she replied, the tears streaming down her cheeks. "I miss you already." She was soft and tender and vulnerable. But what struck me was how unashamed she was about her tears, her affection, and her hope. She was not at all embarrassed, simply honest and unguarded with her feminine heart. And so she was the loveliest creature I had seen in a long time. I was pierced by her beauty.

As I slumped into my seat, I found myself wondering, *Where does all that tenderness and vulnerability and beauty and desire go? Why is it so rare, especially among Christian women?* I realized with deep sadness that few women I know seem to keep their feminine hearts with them into adulthood. I am privileged to know many wonderful women, both from my counseling practice and my work with college students and through my treasured friendships. They are talented, devoted, even self-sacrificing. Yet every one of them shares the same dilemma: a deep and destructive confusion about what it means to be a woman, and especially about what to do with their heart in a world like this.

Walk into church, take a look around, and ask yourself this question: What is a godly woman? Don't listen to what is said; listen to the lives of the women who are present, especially those who are held up as leaders. What are we asking of women? Far too often we're asking them to be tired. As Jan Meyers so honestly admits, "We are far more disciplined than we are at rest, far more committed than winsome, far more 'nice' than passionate, far more dutiful than free. Far more weary than filled with hope." Far more like that haggard mother than her precious little girl.

Brent Curtis and I wrote *The Sacred Romance* in hopes of setting the hearts of people free from a Christianity of duty and obligation, and the response has been simply wonderful. Even still, I have been searching for this book for a long time—a book with the themes of the heart, but specifically for women. Quite honestly, I didn't have anything to recommend to women seeking shelter from the assault of a world that teaches them to be hard and a church that urges them to be efficient. The shelves of our local bookstores are breaking under the weight of books showing women how to be more disciplined, more productive, more loving; how to gain control over their emotions or their eating or their relationships, even over their walk with God. But I simply can't bring myself to buy them, let alone pass them along. I refuse to lay one more burden on the backs of the women I know and care about. I want something to set a woman's heart free.

I have found it.

Jan Meyers has been a close friend and colleague of mine for years. She is one of the few women I know who have learned to keep their hearts alive in a world that gives women every reason not to. She knows the feminine journey, and her counsel has been tested in the fires of reality. I am grateful to say that it is all profoundly true. The proof is in her own life and in the lives of the women she has helped. They are restful, winsome, passionate, and free. They are full of hope. Even as I read the manuscript, I found myself thinking of friends for whom I wanted to make a bootleg copy. Surely that's a sign of a good book.

Now, don't get me wrong—*The Allure of Hope* is not an easy read. It will uncover places in your heart long abandoned, reveal the strategies you've been using to distance yourself from your own femininity, and make the choice before you unmistakably clear. But I doubt you would have read this far if you were still happy with that other way of living and the weariness it induces. And so let me simply encourage you: If you want to take the risk of coming alive as a woman, this book will take you there with grace, with honesty, with humor, and with hope. You will find it . . . alluring. And the effect upon you will be alluring as well.

—JOHN ELDREDGE

Acknowledgments

JAN ESHER. Your friendship birthed this book. Your strength of soul astounds me. I am so grateful for you, beautiful Jan.

❧

DAN ALLENDER. Your impact is woven through the fabric of my life—and woven in this work too much for telling. Thank you for letting God seize you with His love.

❧

BETH ROYAL. My elegant warrior-friend. "The very fabric of you is familiar." You are a gift to me.

❧

JOHN AND STASI. Our lives were thrown together with abrupt kindness. I'm grateful to have friends like you who grieve, listen, wonder, and battle with courage often misunderstood and dependence rarely known.

❧

MY BELOVED COVENANT GROUP. Royals, Hertels, Hendersons, Susan, Bensons, Pinsons, Karla, Heather, Skibas, and Peggy. You've been my landing place and a rare taste of true church.

❧

LORI, LETA, KATY, MICHELE, AND GAYLE. You are the essence of this book.

❧

GINNY. Thank you for caring about me in your grief. You are a generous woman.

❧

BETH STANLEY AND DARLENE HAYES. For years of faithful friendship.

PEGGY HENJUM. Our history began long before we met. Thanks for your labor of love.

❧

CAROLE, TOM, ANDREW, RYAN, AND DANIEL. Thank you for walking with me and always making me a part of your family.

❧

DICK MEYERS. Thanks for your friendship, love, and computer!

❧

MARY AND WALT MEYERS. For your love and lives, thank you.

❧

NANCI MCALISTER. For your belief in this message.

❧

ERIC STANFORD AND LORI MITCHELL, MY EDITORS. Thanks for your kind eyes and patient hands.

❧

To those who took the time to read the manuscript and interact with me about it along the way, thanks. And to all those who have shared their lives with me in friendship, conversation, and the battle for hearts, thank you. To all who prayed with me during moments of opposition, thank you.

❧

Sometimes I think I am the most fortunate woman in the world. The stories held in this book are a reflection of the kind of people I have had the privilege of interacting with both in conversation and in friendship. Most of the identities in these stories have been altered, and many of the counseling scenarios are a blending of several stories in order to maintain confidentiality. I thank all those who gave their permission for their stories to be used.

SOLI DEO GLORIA.

~ 1

THE ACHE THAT
DOESN'T GO AWAY

*Don't tear your clothes in
your grief; instead, tear your hearts.*
—THE LORD

Satan laughed with delight the day the music died.
—DON MCLEAN

*I could no more stop dreaming
than I could make them all come true.*
—DAVID WILCOX

Glare hits my windshield as I drive away from church. I turn
the corner, and my heart sinks. I'm driving away with the same
flat spirit. I am grateful for my church—searched long for it—
so this little corner of God's people can't be responsible for my
malaise. What I'm going through is an all-too-familiar struggle
these days, though. Where is my passion? Where is my exuberance, my winsomeness? I am not feeling terribly lovely these
days; I can't seem to find a settled sense of beauty. I pass the

downtown area and look to the mountains, and they prompt a sudden smile. They stimulate a moment of deep desire and gratitude. I realize this moment is the first time this morning I have been awakened.

I scan through my memories of the morning's happenings, wondering again what it was that started the gnawing at the fringes of my spirit. Was it the conversations at church, which felt predictably rushed? Was it the pleas for more involvement, structured around duty and commitment, going to meetings and catching up on activities? Was it the sermon, instructing us on how to live a life that honors God? Whatever it was, the gnawing is happening again. I am tired. I can't put my finger on what is wrong, but rather than leaving refreshed, I am leaving weary. The morning was filled with lots of movement but little stimulus of soul.

It wasn't always this way. The exuberance of my early days in the knowledge of Christ's love for me lingers in my heart. Everything was new and about Him. Colors were vibrant; music pierced me easily; my heart was tender. I was overwhelmed with the awe of being forgiven; there seemed to be an endless supply of energy of heart to pour into others. My eyes were open to all that was lost. In the truest sense, I was more *female* than I had ever been. I had been awakened, and He had awakened me. As I glance at the snowcapped peak through my car window, I remember those days with sweet longing.

Being awakened by God, sought out by His relentless love despite our wandering, is the heartbeat of Christianity. For a woman, God's pursuit opens places long locked away, places not remembered since childhood. We respond to His advances with the heart of a child, and we live them out on this path called womanhood. Yet something gets lost in the translation. I'm not sure where we've lost it, but as women, we have lost our innocence and our desire.

Most women can think of at least a few moments from their innocence when all felt right with the world, moments before weariness crept in to steal their exuberance. Consider one little girl:

The carpet feels warm underneath the dining room table as she lazily rolls over. Her six-year-old eyes take in the dust specks floating through the sun streaming from the window to her little refuge. She is completely at rest, her mind freely wandering from a conversation with a neighborhood kitten to dreams of her birthday party. Her heart is a vast open place of dreaming, of knights and princes, horses and castles, lakes and sunshine, laughter and love. Her senses remember favorite meadows, bareback horse rides, velvet dresses, willow-tree branches. She hums a tune as she envisions her hero — she can see herself completely abandoned to the pursuit of the knight who comes to release her from her castle. She is beautiful, and she waits for him. She is well occupied as she waits. He will come. She waits for her daddy to be done with his work so she can run into his strong arms. She knows what it is she waits for. She is happy and content to do so; she knows she is not forgotten.

She is every girl. Not every girl knows freedom to this degree; not every girl has a father worthy of such trust — but every woman carries inside her an echo of this winsome spirit.

Why is it just an echo? And why is this echo not resounding, increasing, expanding in the hearts of women who know the love of Christ? We are far more disciplined than we are at rest, far more committed than winsome, far more "nice" than passionate, far more dutiful than free. Far more weary than filled with hope.

How do some women carry their winsome spirit into their adult years despite the jolts and disappointments of life? How is their girlish dreaming transformed into the rich whimsy of a woman's heart? How do they become visionary women, not limited by naïveté and not paralyzed by fantasy? And how do they live above and in the midst of a frenzied church culture that does not seem to stir their hearts?

Six months have passed since she lost the baby. The calendar turns over to another year. She pauses in the hallway by the room that would have been a nursery — now a makeshift office for her husband. They aren't sure how to plan. She weeps a bit, talks with a friend on the phone for a while, then heads into the kitchen to prepare dinner. I'm tempted to hope she will remind herself that time heals all wounds. But more, I find myself drawn to the tenderness of her grief.

She's been with him for twelve years now. As she crawls into bed, trying not to disturb him, she recognizes an ache she often pushes away. She always thought there would be more than this. She's not unhappy. She can't complain. But she feels as though she's been lost somehow, especially in the last year as pressures have mounted and worries about the kids have increased. She pauses for a moment in the dark silence, not knowing what to do with the gnawing emptiness in her heart. I'm tempted to hope she pushes away the ache. But I want more for her too.

She has fought the aggressive brain tumor for two years now. Her husband and daughter have looked on as pain and confusion have wracked her body and mind. "It's not about the cancer," she says to me. "To be consumed with God is all that matters." I'm tempted not to trust her words. But more, I am silenced.

She can feel it happening again. The clerk looked right past her, almost as if she had no face. She needs assistance, so she reaches out to summon the clerk, who is startled to find her there. She wonders again if she'd have to labor so hard at a routine task if she were of a different color. I'm tempted to tell her we all know prejudice. But more, I'm sorry for the blindness.

She heads to the community discussion group with ambivalence. She has come to love these people, all so diverse. They challenge her thinking and her spirituality and her convictions, and she loves the opportunity to let them in on the things that make her tick. They are all married, and she is alone. She feels the familiar twinge shoot through her soul as she thinks of engaging in another community event in a world of couples. I'm tempted to tell her to rise above it, but I understand her ache.

How is it these women have not become hardened? How have their delicate passions not been crushed? How have they continued to live with an openness to other people without discounting or discrediting their own heart's journey? How have they become women who give of their presence without saying a word? Why do I long to be like them?

It is hard—moving into life while carrying around an unmet hope or desire. There is not a woman alive who does not on some level feel the reality of heartache. The dreams born in our girlish wonder pull at the fringes of our hearts, but we push them away as frivolous, impractical, and foolish. How do we live and continue to give of ourselves—honestly, not out of duty but freely—in the midst of feeling a gnawing sense of incompleteness? The apostle Paul said so clearly, "Now these three remain: faith, hope and love. But the greatest of these is love" (1 Corinthians 13:13, NIV). How do we continue to genuinely love those around us in the midst of our own disappointments? I would suggest that love in a woman's heart comes from her level of responsiveness to the hope within her. Hope remembers things lost and envisions things not yet known. Responding to hope causes an ache that doesn't go away.

CHILDLIKE INNOCENCE

"Dear Aunt Jan," the card began.

I really miss you. As soon as I got this card, I started writing. Even in the car. Sometimes, when I listen to soft music, or just sit somewhere wandering off into space, I think of you. I cry until something happens. Now I almost know I'll live in Colorado or New Mexico, because I just can't live without you.

Love, Andrew

17

Created in the freedom of an eight-year-old boy's heart, these words have come to represent more than just gushes from a cherished nephew. These words are a picture of hope, a monument to the fact that having an open heart is possible. Every time I pull this card from its sacred place in my drawer, I'm haunted by the ongoing fight in my own life to keep such a posture of openness. The cynical crust that spreads over my own soul is exposed as I hear the abandon in Andrew's heart.

My nephew's card unwittingly reveals the timeless truth from *The Little Prince:* "It is only with the heart that one can see rightly, what is most important is invisible to the eye."[1] It reveals, too, Jesus' eternal imperative: "The Kingdom of God belongs to such as these" (Mark 10:14). The card embodies what it is to live out of the heart, completely abandoned, unashamed, and open. This is what hope looks like. Words like *pure, open,* and *vulnerable,* and words like *passion, devotion,* and *honesty* come to mind as a child's heart is heard.

So, why do we hesitate to live with such a childlike, open posture? Forgive such an obvious question. It is because we suffer. Each one of us can recall the moment when the childlike, open posture gave way to fear, disbelief, or disillusionment. Or perhaps we understand that living with childlike faith brings the subtle ache that does not go away. The groaning comes from unlimited vision of what could be. Andrew's ability to overwhelm me with his tenderness came directly out of his ache— his ache for me, his vision for our times together, even his dreaming of the western terrain of Colorado or New Mexico.

So, what can we, as women, learn from this fledgling young man? There is an insatiability to a child's soul that reflects the truth that there is always more to discover, always more to dream about. It is rare that we have to remind a child to want more. It is a child's innocence that allows her to open wide the doors of the heart. It is innocence that allows hope. It is life and suffering that birth the ache. There is a groaning to hope the minute innocence is lost.

When did the cards we write turn from whimsy to practicality? When did openheartedness turn to skittishness and timidity? What was being whispered to us as these changes occurred?

As I've spoken to countless women, I've been struck with the words they come up with when asked to think of hope: *anticipation, renewal, expectation, motivation, trust, promise, excitement.* Frankly, we are cowards. Are those descriptions of hope? Absolutely these are threads within hope's fabric. But words like *groaning, yearning, birth pain, anguish, doubt,* and *struggle* don't immediately come to mind. Why? As women, we know these realities intimately. We know what it is to wait. We wait for Daddy's hug. We feel the junior-high anticipation as the phone rings—will it be *him?* We live through nine months of worrying and praying for all to be well with our baby. We wait for our daughter to come home from the prom, wondering how her heart has been handled. We quietly question whether there is enough loveliness in us to keep others engaged with our hearts.

These realities are intrinsic to the nature of hope and woven into the fabric of our souls as women. Hope cannot be separated from its gut realities. We think of hope as something "out there" that we either find or lose. The reality is, hope is something that rises up inside of us with a gentle strength that requires a response. We either respond to it with our hearts or we try to push it down. Responding to it brings a deepened sense of thirst, a deepened ache. Responding to it reminds us of what it truly means to be a woman. Trying to push it down is another story altogether. Notice I said "trying" to push it down. Hope is tenacious. Hope always finds us again.

The apostle Paul reminded a group of Christians in Rome that keeping the childlike heart of hope was . . . well, *glorious.*

You should not be like cowering, fearful slaves. You should behave instead like God's *very own children, adopted into his family—*

calling him "Father, dear Father." For his Holy Spirit speaks to us deep in our hearts and tells us that we are God's children. And since we are his children, we will share his treasure, for everything God gives to his Son, Christ, is ours, too. (Romans 8:15-17, emphasis added)

What confidence. What quiet trust. But then Paul takes us to a more difficult place: "But if we are to share his glory, we must also share his suffering" (verse 17). And then he takes us to the place where childlike whimsy and mature hope collide. It is a place of anticipation, desire, and yearning:

Yet what we suffer now is nothing compared to the glory he will give us later. For all creation is waiting eagerly for that future day when God will reveal who his children really are. Against its will, everything on earth was subjected to God's curse. All creation anticipates the day when it will join God's children in glorious freedom from death and decay. For we know that all creation has been groaning as in the pains of childbirth right up to the present time. And even we Christians, although we have the Holy Spirit within us as a foretaste of future glory, also groan to be released from pain and suffering. We, too, wait anxiously for that day when God will give us our full rights as his children, including the new bodies he has promised us. Now that we are saved, we eagerly look forward to this freedom. For if you already have something, you don't need to hope for it. But if we look forward to something we don't have yet, we must wait patiently and confidently.

And the Holy Spirit helps us in our distress. For we don't even know what we should pray for, nor how we should pray. But the Holy Spirit prays for us with groanings that cannot be expressed in words. (Romans 8:18-26, emphasis added)

BIRTH PAINS

Groaning. The groaning of unsatisfied hearts that long for more. The eighth chapter of Romans paints a clear picture of our groaning. We are described as being in the throes of childbirth, waiting and pushing, anguishing, languishing, the only comfort being the thought that the process will end with the revelation of Christ one day. So, why do we structure our conversations and worship services in a way that denies the reality of suffering?

As I write this, my friend Lori is in labor. Her baby has a mind of her own (she'll surely be a fiery redhead like her mother!) and has been overdue for a week. Lori has been in the hospital since yesterday, and they just induced. Talk about groaning. I just got off the phone with her husband, who is in the birthing room with her. He sounds absolutely wiped out, and the process hasn't even really begun yet. He said, "I've never felt more helpless in all my life. I'm sitting here watching Lori in pain, and there's nothing I can do to help." Hang in there, Matt. It will all be worth it.

Our interactions with one another often resemble the behavior of a father who is too distraught at his wife's suffering to remain in the birthing room — he steps out into the hospital hallway, only to cover his ears to his wife's agony. The baby is coming, the process is long, and the father is checking out long enough to let the suffering subside. When it's all over, *then* he will revel in the baby's presence. Why do we check out? And perhaps more importantly, why do we call our checking out *maturity?* And as women, why do we flee this process that reflects so much of what we know intrinsically anyway?

Why do we insist on telling each other, in ways we perhaps don't intend, that trusting God means making an orderly existence for ourselves, that growing in godliness means we become increasingly satisfied and complete? We tell each other to remember that the suffering will end, but we say these words from hearts that haven't entered the bloody, hot, fierce environment of birth pains. Can our words be trusted?

We leave the birthing room daily. We want freedom from the ache. We want to control the level of groaning in our life. Our search for relief is utterly foolish, yet we demand it with fervor every time we shut off the whispers in our hearts—the whisper to dream, the whisper to acknowledge a current disappointment, the whisper to remember something or someone lost. We desire the thrill of a newborn cry without the months of anticipation and hours of labor-ridden hell.

One of the most treasured scenes from my life occurred on a wet, red-soil road in Swaziland, southern Africa. It was a warm but misty early morning, and I was out for a jog (something that always felt surreal as I would puff by the hordes of lorry drivers on their way to work or pass a woman with a load of timber on her head) when it happened. As I made my way out of town into the hilly countryside, I suddenly heard a distant but piercing sound. It chilled my blood. I stopped jogging. What was that sound? It was unnerving, but so . . . lovely.

Soon I realized I was hearing the sound of a group of women wailing. I saw a small homestead so far in the distance that it was almost indistinguishable from the terrain. But in this homestead a birth was occurring, and the wails were coming not just from one woman but from a gathering of them.

My morning jog had been jolted by the way of life in Africa—entering into another's pain and joy. Wailing is a common occurrence during birth and death. The beauty of the wail comes from a deep sense that says, "We are suffering together. We are a bloody, hot, sticky mess, but we will get through this. As we enter the chaos, we have a deep sense that it really will all end sometime. That is our hope."

Scripture calls Christ in us the hope of glory (Colossians 1:27). Jesus' life was not sterile. He consistently plunged into the unclean places of people's lives and hearts. Not much about it was organized or even made sense. But His life was saturated with vision, and He lived out of a deep sense of mission that propelled Him to take the dusty steps to the most egregious of all birthing places: the cross of Calvary. "He was willing to die a shameful death on the cross," we are told, "because of the joy he knew would be his afterward" (Hebrews 12:2). What was it that He saw? What did He know of the future? What was His hope?

Jesus understood what it would be like for us. He was there in Eden when His Father was compelled to relinquish the sweet communion He had known with the man and woman in the cool of the day. He was there when the Father handed them over to pain in childbirth and futile labor. Jesus understands that our journey is long and arduous. And yet He says this:

> "Truly, you will weep and mourn over what is going to happen to me, but the world will rejoice. You will grieve, but your grief will suddenly turn to wonderful joy when you see me again. It will be like a woman experiencing the pains of labor. When her child is born, her anguish gives place to joy because she has brought a new person into the world. You have sorrow now, but I will see you again; then you will rejoice, and no one can rob you of that joy." (John 16:20–22)

Henri Nouwen said simply that Jesus connects joy with the promise of seeing Him again. I don't know about you, but as I think on these words, my ache increases. That day is coming, but it isn't here yet.

It is a long wait. Hope is far more a waiting for something in a hot, sticky mess than it is a peaceful, orderly affair. No wonder the pulse and tenor of the music originating from Africa's shores, deepened in the shackles of slavery, are rich in hope. Spirituals groan. And spirituals impact the heart in ways similar to the birthing cry: As they release the hope within us, they unnerve us and cause us to feel less comfortable, far more *wanting*, far more *waiting*.

LOSING THE ACHE

So, where has it gone? Where has the freedom to want, ache, and dream gone? If hope produces a deepened desire, an aching waiting, why do we, individually and collectively, speak and act as though maturity means we have become satisfied?

Our own hearts have stacked up the data—scene upon scene of disappointment, betrayal, and confusion that render to us the only conclusion that seems sane: *The groaning will overwhelm me if I even think about the innocence I once knew.*

Gerald May writes of this conclusion:

> *In our society, we have come to believe that discomfort always means something is wrong. We are conditioned to believe that feelings of distress, pain, deprivation, yearning and longing mean something is wrong with the way we are living our lives.*
>
> *Conversely, we are convinced that a rightly lived life must give us serenity, completion and fulfillment. Comfort means "right" and distress means "wrong." The influence of such convictions is stifling to the human spirit. Individually and collectively, we must somehow recover the truth. The truth is, we were never meant to be completely satisfied.*[2]

In a society weary from decades of rationalism, the church is offering little refreshment to souls who are becoming increasingly aware of their thirst for an experience of God. As our culture in this postmodern age slowly awakens to the spiritual yearning within, the church's posture is often one that promises a deliverance from that yearning. In so doing, the church is making a false promise. And this false promise is especially disheartening to women. We know we want our hearts stirred. We want to want. We are just afraid, that's all. We intrinsically know that hope is a painful process. Yet we want to have the courage to respond to hope anyway.

HOPE'S BEGINNINGS

Whether in a place, with a person, or through a sound, smell, or taste, we have all known moments or seasons of abandon and relaxation. Moments that have told us, "All is well." These are the places where we learn that an open heart is possible.

A winsome spirit was born for me in a locale that embodied the strong embrace of God. Repetitively, I was compelled back to one spot—a place on the high canyon wall above the Rio Grande. From my childhood home in northern New Mexico, I could reach this spot on foot in fifteen minutes. These were fifteen minutes spent in an almost priestly preparation for what was to come. Every time, there was anticipation, never any clear sense of what might be unveiled in my trembling, hungry young heart. One thing was certain: this rugged terrain would challenge the frail moorings of my humanity. The softness of its drama would draw me to a place beyond my own worries, desperation, and growing anguish, which had cruelly interrupted my innocence.

Expansive crimson and turquoise skies outlined by mountain peaks on either side—this was the backdrop to my temple. Mountains close enough for my touch until the magnitude of the wild terrain startled me to realize they were eighty miles off, my distant but comfortable companions. Porous, dark volcanic rock formed a comfortable perch, which was my pew. Piñon-laden, high-desert air, my incense. Stillness. Silence. Shadow. The occasional interruption of a hovering hawk, a welcome penetration into the sermon of my soul.

This threshold between mountain splendor and desert wilderness was a place of refuge for me. It didn't offer relief, but it did offer great comfort, an understanding of the wild places into which my heart was asked to travel, even as a young girl. History and future seemed swallowed up in each moment that I lingered on that cliff; the place seemed to tell me that my history and future were not going to engulf me any more than would the river valley. Rather, something of the chiseled beauty around me might actually be built into me, too, if I allowed my heart to respond.

Later in life I read some words of John DeWitt McKee that captured a bit of what this sacred place offered me. "It is unrelenting land," McKee said, "this great, fierce, challenging, canyon-gutted, mesa-muscled land, which holds us and which gives us space enough to write a life on."[3] I was at home there like no place else. It was writing hope in me.

Scenes filled my mind. Childhood curiosity as tree frogs were rallied by my slender fingers from the cracks in the rocks during the spring runoff at the arroyos. Eleven-year-old eyes glimpsing the expanse around me with an "Oh good, you're still there" familiarity. The threat of junior-high hallways giving way to the surrender of the solace that only the Sangre de Cristo mountains could provide in their embrace. In deep nighttime darkness, the landscape provided a young woman a place to weep and wonder as the glittering sky hung low above my hurting and questioning heart.

During my college years, it was the place where my deepest longings dared to surface. Finely honed dreams of romance and marriage—my favorite dream being the moment I would introduce my husband to my canyon spot, seeing his heart hold an equal appreciation of its majesty.

I return to my spot occasionally. I went there a few months ago with new friends, and I wrote these words in my journal: "So amazing. So quiet. So expansive. Beauty unto itself grows stale, but beauty along the way penetrates the heart. The beauty of this place has always been faithful to penetrate my heart along the way."

Along the way it has had the strength to hold the scenes of my life, like liturgy and ritual. Along the way it has nudged me to the conviction that my heart could stay open, my soul alive, even in the face of piercing disappointment, lengthy barren seasons of the soul, an uncertain future. Along the way I'm compelled back to the posture this beauty calls me to, back to the open-hearted stance that such dreaming requires of me.

Hope finds me. It wells up from within and shouts, "It is not the dream itself that is the point. The point is how the dream opens up the weary heart!" Hope uncovers the heart so that it is exposed to the harsh winds of high-desert beauty. Sheltering the heart (refusing to hope) keeps the harsh winds from penetrating but also precludes the chiseled beauty that harsh winds can craft in the hardest of volcanic stone.

HOPE'S INTERRUPTIONS

The New Mexico landscape did indeed open up a weary heart. I was far too weary, far too young for what I was facing.

Innocence is interrupted in all good stories, and my interruptions came as I watched my mother enter what would be a cyclic battle with manic-depression. The first episode I remember came when I was in second grade. Her battle included lengthy hospitalizations, shock treatments, and a suicide attempt. I wrongly determined that it was up to me to keep my mother alive. Where my heart went with all this we'll explore later, but the point is, I was jolted by life's suffering.

The jolts continued as I headed into a future that contained years of singleness I never anticipated. Joy and adventure along the way, yes, but I never imagined living out those adventures while waking up by myself every morning.

And in this current season of life, as suffering has become more of a reality than a threat, I've been humbled again by its entrance. Not too long ago I lost one of my dearest friends and my counseling partner, Brent Curtis, when he was killed in an accident while conducting a men's retreat. And recently I lost a compelling love, along with dreams of marriage and motherhood, in a broken engagement.

The simple fact is, without hope I would not have made it this far. And without hope I wouldn't want to continue. As Brent Curtis and John Eldredge articulated so well in their book *The Sacred Romance,* the arrows of life pierce our innocence and lodge in our hearts with many messages designed to harm us.[4] Hope is what is pierced by these arrows. And hope is the power that transcends those arrows and uses them to expand our vision of God's love.

THE RESTAURANT OF HOPE

Envision an exquisite five-star restaurant. You walk through the door and are gently jolted with the lull of conversation, the warmth of candlelight and luminous nooks, the mingled smells of several fine dishes. The room is festive and relaxing. The maitre d' ushers you to your table, causing you to feel not only welcomed but even expected and desired. You feel the tension drain away as you prepare to enjoy the company at your table and the meal you anticipate as you scan the list of possibilities.

Looking up from your menu for a moment, you glance toward the kitchen and catch the eye of the chef, a kind-looking man. He acknowledges your gaze with a warm smile and a look that, in your restful state, says to you, "I am preparing something wonderful just for you. Wait. You'll love it. I'm doing this for you." You feel a twinge of embarrassment, but it is quickly engulfed in the sheer delight of thinking that something is being prepared with you in mind.

You love this place. Life feels right for a moment, and you take it all in. How could he have known what you love? You wait and converse and laugh and drink and wait. And then it arrives—the spectacular dish. All are served, and with gratitude you savor your first bite. Heaven. Perfection. How did he do this? You continue to imbibe and laugh, and time slips away. . . .

Suddenly, a tap on your shoulder. Startled, you turn to see the maitre d' standing behind you with a grim look on his face. "I'm sorry, but I have to ask you to leave." You are certain there is an emergency and you request the details, but none are given. "No, I simply must ask you to leave. Please come with me." His voice is commanding and direct. You are stunned and embarrassed but feel compelled to follow, at least to see what this interruption is about. The maitre d' ushers you past tables of glowing faces and candles, then through the kitchen, where you look for the chef but see only busboys. You are taken out the back door into the frigid night air, down the cement steps and into the alley behind the restaurant. Furious and confused, you demand an explanation, but all that is given in reply is the turn of the deadbolt lock.

Silence.

You are stunned. You are alone. Trash cans, oily puddles, and the steam from a sewer vent make up your new surroundings. Welcome to the alleyway.

The most natural thing for us to do when we have been jolted into the alleyway by life is to think, *This is where my hope is lost. My sweet dream has been snatched away, and hope has been snatched away with it.* The wild reality of God, though, is that this is where hope begins. Hope begins when the memory of *what was* becomes a longing for *what is to be restored.*

This is the place where contemplating a posture of openness and childlike dreaming seems utterly ridiculous. This is where the journey of the heart can easily be indicted as foolish. And indeed, it is foolish—a foolishness that leads to life. It is the kind of outlandish living that Paul spoke of when he said we are fools for Christ's sake (1 Corinthians 4:10).

TOO GOOD TO BE TRUE

The bitter winds that penetrate us in that first cruel step into the alleyway of disappointment provide us with a choice. What will we do with our hearts now that betrayal and loss of control have seemingly shown themselves more powerful than any loving glance or pleasurable, savory bite of a meal? There are three general choices we can make when surrounded by the cold concrete of the alley (sometimes I make all three choices within a single day): First, we can give in to resignation and self-contempt (I call it "hovering"—see chapter 2). Next, we can become more determined and driven (I call it "clamoring"—see chapter 3). Last, we can choose to keep our hearts open and focused on the only sure future God has promised us (God calls it "hope").

The meal is unique for each of us. My meal is one of being told, "It's not up to you, you know. I'll take care of it. Please rest. I see you. I see how hard you're trying, and you don't need to try so hard. Do you not see how deeply enjoyable you are even when you aren't keeping someone alive?" How my young heart yearned to hear words like that. I heard them whispered to me on the canyon wall. They were words that seemed too good to be true.

That's the nature of the meal, after all. It seems too good to be true. But deep in our female souls exists a yearning to hear the voice that says, "I see you. Your loveliness is intoxicating. Your heart is full and substantial, and I am drawn to know you. I see your confusion, stubbornness, and darkness, and I will not back away. You are not too much for Me. You are deeply enjoyable, and you are safe here. There's so much more of you to know; I can't wait to know all of you. And you can never know all of Me. I can't wait to shelter you and release you to flourish."

It is the uninvited phone calls, diseases, rapes, repeatedly unmet requests, severed friendships, infertility, singleness, lost passion, wayward children, or the sheer repetition of life—it is these that take us into the alleyway, putting us in a place of either responding to or pushing down hope. These assaults seem to mock the meal itself. But it is in the alleyway that the promise of Ezekiel 14:5 is realized. God begins to deal with us according to the things we are trusting in, in order to recapture our hearts.

The question for us as women is, can we have eyes to see the redemptive purposes in the alleyway? Can we trust that God has not forgotten us and that in fact He has intentions for us in the alleyway that go beyond our wildest imaginings? He wants our hearts. And it is in the alleyway that He can get our attention long enough to prove it.

~ 2

THE PATH OF HOVERING

From now on, you and the woman will be enemies.
—GOD TO THE SERPENT

There is no new frontier. We have got to make it here.
—DON HENLEY

I sit alone inside myself and curse my company, for this thing that has kept me alive so long is now killing me.
—BOB BENNETT

When the interruptions come into our lives, some things are immediate. Like the way we call God into question. We carry with us Eve's legacy, and it doesn't take much for us to be "convinced," just as she was, by the serpent (Genesis 3:4-6). Eve was convinced God was withholding something from her. Colors more vivid than aquamarine, turquoise, evergreen; aromas more pungent than eucalyptus, honeysuckle, magnolia; textures beyond silk and satin—this extravagance didn't compel her to remember the true story God had given to her and to Adam. Constant exploration and freedom didn't keep her attention. She didn't check out the facts with Adam. The serpent's whisper of accusation against the heart of God was enough for her to be convinced. She didn't want to be left out if there was more.

And she was in the garden! The lavish meal or the hints of abandon we have known are only feeble echoes of that place. The garden wasn't enough to keep her heart satisfied. And we are called to keep our hearts open in a dreary alley? As my five-year-old friend Jacob would say, "Yeah, *right.*"

It's very subtle, isn't it? We spend our retirement money and still face infertility. We muster up the courage to go to singles groups and dinner clubs, and we still haven't found a spouse. We get to the top of our form in the career and homemaking juggle, only to find that a disease has crept into our family. We invest untold energy in our child's life, and he decides to run away from home. We hear the whispers of the serpent, and our hearts are convinced. We say, "Surely God doesn't care for me if He allowed me to be dropped into *this* mess! Surely I can see that His care is quite limited, not exactly what He told me. I've been duped by this God of mine. How cruel of Him to taunt me this way!"

As we join hands with Eve and are convinced, we begin to make choices, following in her footsteps. Gerald May says we naturally seek the least-threatening ways of trying to satisfy our longing for God, ways that protect our sense of personal power and require the least sacrifice.[1] Exactly. For women, the first choice is the path of hovering.

Choosing this path shows an immediate resignation to the realities of the dark alleyway behind the Restaurant of Hope; there is a finality to it, as far as we're concerned. Our thoughts run along these lines: *Oh, great. I knew it. I could have predicted this. It was too good to be true, anyway, that fine meal. Who was I trying to kid? It is harsh and cold, and I have to do something soon before the elements destroy me. Well, here's a heating vent. I'll cover myself with these discarded blankets and my coat, sit on the heating vent, and hover here. At least I know how to keep myself alive. I will not be a fool and be reminded of what I just left. I will cover my eyes. I'll shield myself from the aroma of warm food.*

Listen to the voices of resignation, self-contempt, and fear as they whip through the alleyway.

THE VOICE OF RESIGNATION

The first voice, the voice of resignation to the situation, sounds like this: *I could have predicted this! I have got to do something before the elements get to me. At least I know how to keep myself alive.*

It is cold out there. The wind whips through the alleyway with biting force. Bits of trash swirl in the center of the alley. It is a quick decision, really. No time to concern yourself with what just happened; hurry and cover up. Remember only that you have the ability to come up with all kinds of creative ways to survive.

As my mom's depressions grew darker and more unpredictable, I made a determination. It wasn't conscious, exactly. I was frightened. I had to come up with some alternative to watching this tender woman destroy herself. Her threats of taking her life were too much for me. So, somewhere in my second-grade year, I began to talk to Mom about her problems. She seemed to appreciate it, and when I was talking to her, the chaos seemed to drain away for both of us. For hours we would sit on the couch, where she would revisit old wounds and share confidences. It never crossed my mind that I was having adult conversations. It never crossed my mind that I was carrying a weight far too great for my age. I found that these talks could convince her to stay alive one more day, and that's all I knew to want.

My childhood whimsy slowly took a turn into a hovering determination: I would keep my mother alive. I would come up with some way to sustain her. I would somehow stay a few steps ahead of my own heart and keep my mother alive. This determination became my blanket. I had found the way to keep myself alive. The truth that my blanket was suffocating my little girl's heart was of course lost to me. I had found my own shelter, and I would now work hard to keep it firmly intact.

THE VOICE OF SELF-CONTEMPT

After resignation has had its say, self-contempt speaks up. It says, *I am such a fool. When am I going to learn not to get my hopes up?*

Hope is our enemy—or at least we make it seem so. What follows may seem like a trite example, but responding to hope is difficult not only in intense suffering but also in something as comical as what happened to us at my friend Beth's wedding. She planned for her bridesmaids to assist her in tying tulle bows onto the ceremony programs. There were three hundred bows to tie. We began two days before the wedding and made a party out of it. Tying bows, swapping stories, dreaming for Beth—the usual wedding party reverie. It was slow going. I think we all secretly wondered if we'd ever get them done in time.

That night we came back to the house and found the table cleared of all our handiwork. No programs, no tulle, no scissors, no bows. We looked around the house and found nothing. We decided that Beth's aunt and cousin had taken pity on us and had taken the project upon themselves, back at their hotel room, so that the wedding party could do other wedding party things. We were all grateful. There was a collective sigh of relief.

The day of the wedding, we were leisurely getting ready, everyone pampering themselves with just a little more effort than usual. We watched Beth pack; we laughed; we were thoroughly enjoying her day. Then her mother came into the room with an ashen face. She held the big bag that contained— you guessed it—all the untied programs. It had been placed behind a door somewhere, and she had just found it.

The reaction was immediate: *How could we have been so stupid?*

We should have known! You can imagine the frantic scramble. We got them done; they looked great and the wedding was beautiful. But at that moment when we discovered the truth, we felt ridiculous for having relaxed. We felt embarrassed for assuming.

AS NATURAL AS BREATHING

I've heard this voice, the voice of self-contempt, for several months as I've been recovering from my broken engagement. I have waited thirty-five years to give my heart, and this man was worth the wait and the risk. I have a circle of friends who know me well, and there was applause as this courtship took off. Obviously there's a context to the story, but the point is, we aren't going to be married. Daily I find myself thinking, *You fool, you knew it was too good to be true. Happy endings and happy beginnings only happen for other people.* I've learned enough through the years to not entirely give in to this, but why am I tempted to make myself the enemy? Why are you tempted to call yourself a fool when you are disappointed?

When our hearts are crushed, don't we immediately feel like fools? It's as natural as breathing, really. Proverbs 13:12 says, "Hope deferred makes the heart sick." I think something got lost in the translation. Shouldn't it say, "Hope deferred makes you feel like your insides just got blown up by a time bomb"? This being true (and I'm assuming you agree it is), why in the world would we want to hope? Why would we not think ourselves nuts for having opened ourselves up to such insanity?

This is why I make myself the enemy. As my fiancé and I part ways, are there relational things I need to consider and own? Absolutely. But as with any other pain, it is always easier to focus on what you can change than to face the questions welling up in your heart in the sorrow of what is beyond your control. I can't change the circumstances. I can't change his mind or his heart. And this leaves me in a place of deep questioning. It leaves me heartsick with hope deferred, and with the temptation to make myself the enemy so I don't have to ache.

I told a woman recently that it felt like she was taking a paintbrush and was globbing black paint all over herself with it. She knew exactly what I was saying. She was finding all kinds of things wrong with her so she could concentrate on fixing them. As she realized what she was doing, she said, "At least I know how to clean myself up. I don't know how to fix my sorrow right now." This is why self-contempt is the path of least resistance when our hearts are bruised. If we can find something about ourselves to get to work on, we are in control. This is why hope calls us away from mocking ourselves, and why it calls us into a deep place of trust.

THE VOICE OF HOVERING FEAR

Along with resignation and self-contempt, fear speaks to us in the alleyway: *I have to do something!* it says. *I have to find a way to cover myself.*

Women are experts at staying ahead of their own hearts. The immediate popularity of Alanis Morrisette's music among both adolescent girls and middle-aged women reflects our hovering with a jagged edge. I've heard some women say she strikes a chord with their anger. I wonder if, really, under all that brazenness, she speaks far more to our fear. In "The Doctor" she says this:

I don't want to be your filler if the void is solely yours

I don't want to be your glass of single malt whiskey hidden in the bottom drawer, and I don't want to be your bandage if the wound is not mine—lend me some fresh air

I don't want to be adored for what I merely represent to you

I don't want to be your baby-sitter; you're a very big boy now

*I don't want to be your mother—I didn't carry you in my womb
for nine months*

Show me the back door . . .

We are so afraid, aren't we? We know precisely what it is we
want from relationships. We want to be filled, but we don't
want to be smothered. We want to be adored, but we don't want
to be idolized. We want to offer care, but we don't want to be
responsible. We want the garden without the Fall.

As our hearts hover, we fearfully tell ourselves that those "too
good to be true" things will never happen for us. We are certain
of our impending disappointment, and we will do anything to
beat to the punch the people we love. Hear the determination as
we say, "They will not get the best of me again." We determine
to cover over the tender yearning to be entered, chosen, lavished
upon. We cover it over with our contempt for ourselves and for
those who try to love us and fail. Our words become Alanis's
words—our hearts long to ask, but we don't. We bite and
devour instead. We become brazen when we are actually scared
out of our wits.

THE VOICE OF FORGETFULNESS

I will shield myself from memory. As we huddle in the warmth of
the heating vent, this is the message formed in our minds by the
temptation to forget.

Frederick Buechner writes of a dream he once had in which
he went traveling through a splendid countryside. He happened
upon a beautiful inn and decided to check in for the evening.
He was delighted as the bellman opened the door to his
room—it actually took his breath away. Everything about this
room seemed to fit him. The bay window overlooked rolling
green hills and water and wildlife. The colors were perfect. The
air was fresh and inviting. There was a huge leather easy chair in

which he could unwind and smoke his pipe with full relaxation. In fact, everything about this room gave him pleasure. He was fully at ease in a way he had never known before.

He left this special inn and went wandering for a time through the countryside. On his return, he of course came back with great anticipation to the place that had given him such surprising joy. Eagerly he went to check in, and the bellman showed him to another room. *No matter,* he thought. *I'm sure they are all the same.* As he walked into this second room, he again was caught off guard, but this time with a sense of deep disappointment. He couldn't put his finger on it, but the room just wasn't the same. The colors were the same, but they seemed dreary somehow. The bay window was the same, but it was slightly smudged and unclear. The air was stale. He sat in the leather easy chair, and it had just the smallest lump in it.

At this point he had to make a decision. He had conversations with himself, trying to convince himself that this second room really wasn't so bad and he should just live with it. But the haunting memory of that first, perfect room was too much for him to bear, so he overcame his embarrassment and pride and went to the front desk.

He told the desk clerk that he couldn't recall the number, but there was this room, and could they manage to place him in that room again? The desk clerk smiled knowingly and asked him if he knew the name of the room. The name? No, he didn't even know the number. The desk clerk continued smiling and told Frederick that he did know of this room, and he would certainly take him back to it. As they approached the door of the first room and set down the luggage, the desk clerk said, "Mr. Buechner, the name of this room is Remember." Puzzled, Frederick walked across the threshold into that first room. The sheer delight of being back in a room so perfect caused him to wake up from his dream.[2]

Without the memory of that first room, we look around the stale existence we're in now and make the best of it so that our hearts are not stirred with desire for that room to be restored to us. Without the memory of Eden, there is no reason for us to feel uncomfortable in this place so marred and filled with the stench of the Fall. It is Eden's memory that invites our hearts to faith (Hebrews 11 offers multiple examples of people who remembered what had been, so that their hearts would gain strength for the present), and it is Eden's memory that invites our hearts to hope. We eagerly desire the day when our memory will be not restored but surpassed as we are ushered into a place prepared for us: a new heaven, a new earth, a place that will cause this cold, stale room to be forgotten (Isaiah 65:16). Blaise Pascal reasoned that faith is the memory of the past and that hope is the memory of the future. We are suspended here, with love being the only power to hold up our hearts. This leaves us with few options in the meantime, really — it is either have memory, have vision, and be about the business of living and loving, or else be done with it. If only the choice were so clear to us.

SO CLOSE

This stale room looks a bit like the first room, doesn't it? Hike up one of Colorado's fourteen-thousand-foot peaks into the windswept tundra and watch the marmots scramble into the rocks. Or take a stroll at Montaña de Oro in California and watch the surf pound onto the rocks and the breeze sweep through the lilac and yellow fields of flowers. Breathe in the foliage of autumn in the East as you drive to Watkins Glen in New York State and hike into a canyon chiseled by water and ice. Have an uproarious laugh with some of your dear friends and think to yourself, *Where did* that *come from?* Eden just showed up in the reverie. Experience an abandoned and connected time of lovemaking with your husband and feel the pulse of God's heartbeat. Find the smallest translucent flower in the concrete cracks of the alleyway and see that Eden showed up in a sigh.

Eden showed up, but it's not *here*.

We're told that Christ in us is the hope of glory (Colossians 1:27). The Spirit of Christ in us is the foretaste of eternity and a memory of the garden. This foretaste was meant to cause us to hunger for more *and* sustain us in the meantime. When I see a woman living this out—when I see a woman drinking in every taste of life she can without becoming resigned, contemptuous, or fearful—she makes me thirst for God and reminds me that I'll be okay with an open heart.

GYMNASTICS OF THE HEART

Years ago I was struck by a line in a poem by Ruth Bell Graham: "God, let me be all he ever dreamed of loveliness and laughter."[3] What would happen if this wish came true? How many of us know that the men we love, the friends we have, think of belly laughs and compelling conversation when they think of us? Are we thought of with delight and as someone to be taken seriously?

At our best, we've all had a glimpse of it. We all know how exhilarating it is to walk away from an interaction with others and know they are lingering in it because of us. They are smiling. They are thinking. They have been aroused by our presence. These moments are a foretaste of who we are meant to be. But we know there is so much more of us that somehow doesn't make it to our carpools and business meetings and even our lunches with friends. So often our loveliness and laughter are shrouded by a blanket.

A woman who "is clothed with strength and dignity" and who "laughs with no fear of the future" (Proverbs 31:25) is one who, in the alleyway, sees her foolish choice to hover. She realizes her hovering reveals her lack of trust that God will remember her or care about her situation. She admits the Fall actually happened to her own heart. She doesn't try to pretend her heart is full of trust. Instead, she takes her fear, her doubt, and her questions to the God of the universe. She allows herself to respond to God's pursuit. He finds her there, redeems her there, loves her there—so she can look to the future with confident expectation.

Peggy is clothed with strength and dignity. When I met her, she had just been surprised (that's an understatement) by the news that she was pregnant with her fifth child. I was struck by her courage. She and Jim hadn't planned this one, and yet suddenly the road of parenthood stretched out further than she had ever imagined. Shortly after this news, Peggy and Jim were jolted with the discovery that Jim had an advanced form of malignant melanoma. His life was in the balance. I watched with awe as Peggy was ushered into their dark alleyway and faced it with an open heart. She did not pretend all was well. She did not espouse anything trite concerning God's goodness. She admitted that this was the last place she ever wanted to be, and she struggled with her own heart and her God. They fought the disease. She gave to Jim and her children out of her own pain, and her beauty only seemed to deepen as she brought her bewildered heart to the table—with Jim, with friends, with God.

Cancer took Jim's life. Peggy is raising five children without him. She has horrible stretches where it is all too much. And she has days of actual enjoyment. But what astounds me about Peggy is her constant awareness of other people. She always inquires of me with such genuine curiosity and knowledge. There is no sense that she is fleeing her own suffering by focusing on others. That's what is so powerful—she focuses on others in the midst of her own heart's journey. She is not trying to make it happen, but her life laughs at the future. She gives my heart strength to smile at the days to come.

THE ARTISTRY OF BEING A WOMAN

What blocks this kind of beauty from happening in more than just glimpses? It is the way we try to jump over the Fall in our own hearts. We find all kinds of ways to maneuver around the truth that when we left the garden we left with only an echo of beauty, and we left with a curse that we would know pain in childbirth and that our desire would be for control.

As women, we *will* give birth. All of us. Peggy is giving birth to beauty in the midst of extreme circumstances. At all times we are becoming greater reflections of either Eve's design (the beauty and goodness she was created with), or we are reflecting her foolishness (a spirit of control). If we, outside the garden, are reflecting Eve's design, it is happening only because of the power of redemption.

So, what was it like for them? Adam and Eve were both called to subdue and rule over the garden (Genesis 1:26-31). Literally, this meant Eve had been commissioned to take authority over the life growing inside the garden. She was called to shape beauty. She was called to be an artist. Her medium was vast—flowers and forests and soils and aromas beyond comprehension. She had an artistic companion in Adam, and God took full pleasure in their combined handiwork as they walked together in the cool of day. She and Adam spent their days investigating, exploring, and pondering the commission they both had to fill this grand place—to multiply.

Eve was called, from the beginning, to bear fruit from relationship. This was the other arena of her artistry—she was Adam's companion, his "helper" (a prized word used of God when Psalm 46:1 says He is "always ready to help in times of trouble"). Her presence completed the picture, and yet together they were to complete the picture on an ongoing basis. The palette always changing, they were to create with the full companionship and pleasure of the Creator.

This is what was lost. When Eve was convinced, the artistry of being a woman took a fateful dive into the barren places of control and loneliness. Dan Allender says that what was born in a woman's heart at this point was a refusal to bear loneliness and desire. The curse, as it fell on a woman's soul, involved pain in childbirth and a desire to control (literally, to jump out and devour) her husband (Genesis 3:16). From that point on, a woman could choose to enter her loneliness and desire and be an artist in her suffering, or she could flee those heart realities and attempt to control her surroundings, her relationships, her God.

HUMANITY AT ITS FEMININE BEST

You may not know this, but Christianity isn't meant to make you into an efficient, moral woman. Are we meant to change as Christ stuns us with His forgiveness? Absolutely. But the transformation that comes, impacting who we are as women, does so naturally as an afterthought of God's love for us, surprising us as it shows up. Our femininity, our artistry, is transformed—perhaps *released* is a better word—as our hearts are captured by the goodness of God in the midst of our hard-heartedness. If we attempt to be more feminine—if we strive to make "being a godly, feminine woman" our goal—we end up having the feel of a Barbie doll at a dance. Others around us are fluid and laughing. We are stiff and uninviting.

We can't think about our femininity without remembering that there is a battle raging over us. Notice I said "over" us. The battle is all about our hearts. I am not talking about culture wars incited by us—feminism versus antifeminism. I am talking about the scheme of the Evil One, the enemy of women (Genesis 3:15), to shroud God's substance in us. We were meant to live from glory to glory with unveiled faces (2 Corinthians 3:18). But instead, we live from function to function, errand to errand, addiction to addiction, and we are taken in by evil's whisper: "There's more for you as a woman, but God has left you out here in the alley, so you had better take care of yourself."

Gail Wynand, the contemptuous publisher in Ayn Rand's *The Fountainhead,* speaks to this whisper: "If you make people perform a noble duty, it bores them. If you make them indulge themselves, it shames them. But combine the two—and you've got them. . . . Make them itch and make them cry—and you've got them."[4] The Evil One attempts to shroud our femininity not so much by drawing us into obvious sin but by giving us what we ask for in our hovering—giving us noble duties we can control, giving us addictions we can get lost in. Brent said so well,

The core of Satan's plan for each of us is not found in tempting us with obvious sins like shoplifting or illicit sex. These things he uses more as maintenance strategies. His grand tactic in separating us from our heart is to sneak in as the Storyteller through our fears and wounds we have received from Life's Arrows. He weaves a story that becomes our particular "message of the arrows." Counting on our vanity and blindness, he seduces us to try to control life by living in the smaller stories we all construct to one degree or another. He accuses God to us and us to God.[5]

Recently a group of high-profile Christian women met locally. They were called together by one who is well known for her influential teachings on womanhood. Graciously, she wanted to get a sense of where women's needs were, where the direction of her work should head in order to address those needs. My friend Leigh attended this meeting along with about twenty others. Each woman had a chance to say what she thought was important. Leigh heard them say things like "Women are not disciplined enough. We try so hard to motivate them, but they don't have the skills to structure their lives to benefit from it." Another said, "We need to find a way to convince women they have something to give." Leigh patiently waited as woman after woman spoke of commitment and obligation, cheerleading women into enthusiasm.

Leigh began to deflate. She was becoming disturbed; something grievous was going on here. Then she realized that there was no lack in what was being said. She realized she was hearing everyone speak of being well on their way and needing to find a way to assist those who aren't. Leigh thought, *I was a spiritual orphan who found a home in the heart of an older woman who*

*loved me. That's where the love of Christ took root. I come here
today with great need. We all have great need, and we need to meet
each other in the heart in order for God's love to take root.*

When all had spoken their peace, one woman realized they
hadn't heard from Leigh. "Leigh," she asked, "would you like to
add something?"

"Yes," Leigh said with misty eyes. "Isn't all of this missing
the point? I tried for years to be a dutiful, sacrificial Christian
woman, and I always ended up feeling like all the activity was
missing the point. I've realized in the last few years that our
relationship with God is all about Him finding our hearts, and
women are experts at keeping their hearts locked away. How
can we know the joy of forgiveness if we don't see how hard
our hearts are? How can we respond passionately to pleas for
more involvement if our hearts aren't in it? I think we do an
incredible disservice to women by adding to their burden
rather than meeting them where their hearts are, in what they
are thirsty for. Do we want to create women who are more
active, or do we want to multiply women who are desperately
thirsty for the heart of God?"

The room was silent, the other women remembering their
hearts for a moment. It was clear where the beauty was in the
room.

BEAUTY UNVEILED

A gentle and quiet spirit has a natural, earthy beauty. It is
human. It has the power to win others to belief in the goodness
of God (1 Peter 3:4-6). It comes from a vulnerable posture that
surrenders all fear of how a man or anyone else will handle us.
This vulnerable woman has admitted she has been ushered from
the garden; she has entered her desire and loneliness and is looking for God there.

Hannah displayed her yearning without shame as she pleaded
with God for a baby. She was a spectacle, really, crying in her

anguish. Eli the priest thought she was drunk. She allowed her desire to take her to a place of full surrender of the very thing she longed for. When Samuel was born and weaned, she gave him over to God's service (1 Samuel 1). This woman was abandoned to the higher purposes of God but allowed the desires of her heart and her loneliness to *take her* to that abandon.

In the midst of a dating relationship, a woman I know was feeling particularly smug. It seemed to her the man just wasn't seeing what she was bringing to the relationship ("Does he really see who I am? I am so afraid of him not seeing me"). At a particularly hard moment, she heard God whisper, "Squander your beauty." She wasn't sure she heard correctly. Surely God didn't want her to be codependent. "Squander your beauty and trust Me." He doesn't ask much, does He? But hear again. He never asks for more blind sacrifices. He is always asking for more of our heart. How could she possibly give her beauty to a man she wanted to control without God holding her heart as she did so?

The picture painted in Proverbs 31 used to make me tired. I could never be that woman, so why bother? Then I realized that this beautiful proverb is written about a woman who is confident in something other than herself. She is well cared for. She doesn't use the care she's receiving to foster slothfulness. She is a warrior—strong, dignified, undergirded with mission. But she remembers the call to be an artist, and she goes about it on this side of the garden with courage as she remembers who is taking care of her. Her nobility of spirit flows from a conviction that she cannot take care of herself.

All of these women are human. There is an earthy surrender to them. They don't have much to prove; they simply know what they desire. They know what they are asking for. Being at home within our own skin as women causes us to be vulnerable, wild, courageous, strong, playful, thirsty, and noble. No room for religious niceties. These women have guts. They are living life, and as they do so, they are luminous reminders of Eden.

ARTISTS OR OLYMPIANS

A woman attempting to jump over the curse in her own heart can be recognized by her lack of humanness. Is she rigid, extremely controlled in her manner? Does she speak of her "contentment" in a way that is put on rather than flowing from a deep place of rest? Does she seem to be trying to convince her own heart that she really is content, that God really is good? Does she have an extreme need to live within the lines in her relationships? Is she silent (not quiet, silent—having nothing to offer)? Is she saccharin, syrupy? Is she determined to be known as a godly woman? This woman is living with the conviction that she can be Eve without bearing the mark of Eve's failure to trust God's goodness. She's determined to restore the garden herself—no blood sacrifice required, unless it is her own.

Contrast the above with a woman who has fully faced the curse, who has faced her own desperate need. This woman realizes that the pain of desire and loneliness really isn't the issue; it's that her own heart has wandered far from home, far from the sufficient companionship of the Father, far from the artistic call deep within. This woman displays qualities that proclaim her frailty and inability to jump over the curse. She faces the curse on an ongoing basis by allowing her heart to be stirred by desire and by feeling the ache of loneliness. She allows these fruits of the curse to carry her to her heavenly Father with broken vulnerability. She admits to Him how convinced she is that her desire could be sufficiently touched by anything other than His love. She pours out her broken and thirsty heart to Him in ways that mysteriously release a fragrance no amount of religion could conjure up.

THE IRONY OF WANTING MORE

There is a memory of that perfect room in every heart. For us, that memory is one of perfect rest, exploration, adventure, and companionship. It holds a complete sense of being delighted in, protected, and enjoyed. Questions of our loveliness weren't asked in that room. We were goddesslike, and we were secure in our belovedness. Karen Lee-Thorpe and Cynthia Hicks call this "the memory of Eve."[6] We walked with God and with Adam in the cool of the day, carrying on conversations, telling stories of that day's adventures, having an ever-increasing sense of contentment *and* desire. There was always more to know, always more to see, touch, taste, experience. Can you imagine? We knew God was beyond our full knowing, and Adam was there as an ever-present explorer of our beauty. It was all unfolding with increased desire. Eve took it all in with an anchored trust, a mysterious spirit, a compelling soul, and a luminous countenance.

We were brought out of that perfect room because of our rebellion. We were convinced. We allowed our hearts to be seduced by the voice of evil, inviting us to reduce God's lavish gift to one particular place that was off limits—proof positive of God's ill intent toward us. We chose the Tree of the Knowledge of Good and Evil because we couldn't bear being left out. And now the only hope of getting back in comes from God's promise to find us, which He fulfilled on a hill (devoid of beauty) called Golgotha, where His own Son shed His blood to guarantee our restoration into perfect beauty.

What wild irony! Eve thought there could be more, and she was ushered out with her man, cherubim firmly in place to block her return. This place—this alleyway of humanity, this stale room for a woman's heart—becomes the very place where God invites us to remember that there *was* more. And there *will be* more. Our desire for more (the very thing that got us in trouble) becomes the place through which God finds our hearts. He turns our desire on its head to reveal to us that everything we want as women is found in Him. All we can be as women is found in Him.

This truth was learned by the woman who anointed Jesus' feet. She had no reputation to uphold; she'd lost that already.

She was known as an immoral woman, and from the sounds of it, the religious leaders could talk in detailed descriptions about the nature of her sin. She was not sure how to approach Jesus, but she knew she needed Him. As she humiliated herself in the home of a Pharisee, she poured out expensive perfume and wept at His feet, kissing them and wiping them with her hair. All cultural and religious protocol was broken as she brought to Jesus the only things she had: her heart's desire and her heart's beauty. She squandered both in the sight of many eyes filled with disdain. But Jesus' eyes were filled with a different light. He made it clear that her ability to love Him so openly came from her keen awareness of her need and from her depth of gratitude for forgiveness.

This woman had a desperate need for Jesus, prompting Him to say, "I tell you, her sins—and they are many—have been forgiven, so she has shown me much love. But a person who is forgiven little shows only little love" (Luke 7:47). How would this woman fare at a weekly women's meeting or church picnic? A woman who jumps over the curse misses the embarrassment and misses the glory of love. The woman spoken of in Luke 7 is a hero to me because she was willing to risk having people look askance at her in order to ask something of God.

Our relationship with the Deceiver, the enemy of women (Genesis 3:15), impacts how much we respond to the hope in our hearts. If we deny his voice—the voice of resignation, self-contempt, and fear—then we move through the curse into a place of hope. Putting aside the gymnastics of our heart, we rest in a place that turns to the heart of God. "Let me rest in Your strength," we pray. "Let me be desperate in Your presence. Let me give life. Find me in spite of my wandering heart, and please speak on my behalf." That's the way out of the useless hovering response to the alleyway.

3

THE PATH OF CLAMORING

I am, and there is none besides me.
—BABYLON

Never again will you be the
lovely princess, tender and delicate.
—GOD TO BABYLON

We, who with unveiled faces all reflect
the Lord's glory, are being transformed
into his likeness with ever-increasing glory.
—THE APOSTLE PAUL

When asking "What do I do with my heart now?" the first
choice is hovering and the second choice is clamoring. The spirit
of this second choice is obvious in Hollywood, Aspen, Milan,
Manhattan — places where image is everything. But for women
it shows up as we stand before the mirror in the morning, as we
climb into and out of our sweats or slip on our silk blouse, and
somehow we don't feel comfortable with ourselves.

Clamoring calls to us when we don't feel at home in our own

skin. It shows up as we glance over to the car in the next lane and see a mother with three children in a van who looks so good—so perky and energetic—and we feel so pale. It calls to us in a small group as another woman shares her heart and we become frustrated that we aren't like her. We feel it as our husband backs away from us in a heated discussion and we are tempted to bear in harder just to stay connected. Or we try to second-guess what will keep him interested, and we become what it is he's looking for. Where we question our beauty and feel pressured to alter ourselves in order to keep relationship— there is no greater place of confusion for us as women.

If hovering under our self-made blanket in the alleyway seems too tame, clamoring calls us to charge up the steps, pound on the door, and demand our lost meal. Hallmarked by constant movement, both internally and externally, this choice unleashes a frenetic energy to force our way back into hope's restaurant. We will not be left out, left behind, or left without an explanation. Our hectic thoughts sound like this: *Oh no they don't! . . . I belong in that restaurant. . . . At least I thought I did. . . . I have to be in there or I will die. . . . Besides, I deserve to be in there, don't I? . . . I will run up those steps and pound on the door until I'm let back in. . . .*

Can you hear, under all that bravado, a fear that we will be found out—a fear that what we've secretly suspected just may be true, that we never belonged in that fine place to begin with. We were never lovely enough or substantial enough to be in there. We try to figure out what it is they are looking for in their patrons and become whatever it is they want. *I only hope they don't look at me too closely and discover that I am a fraud. I'll keep myself so occupied with how I will gain access to the restaurant that I never have to be reminded of the meal nor the kind look in the chef's eyes.* And all of this is based on the question, Do I have enough beauty to keep relationship?

There's been a song floating through the airwaves recently in which a poor guy laments how unworthy he is of the goddess he's just met. "She's so high above me, she's so lovely. She's so high like Cleopatra, Joan of Arc, or Aphrodite," he sings. He's convinced she'll never give him the time of day—such is the intoxicating power of her beauty. Billy Joel tells us, "She can kill with a smile, she can wound with her eyes. Blame it all on yourself 'cause she's always a woman to me." Shania Twain says she feels like a woman in men's shirts and short skirts. So, which is it? All of these images capture a glimpse of our beauty's power, but we kind of know—don't we?—that a thousand top-twenty hits (or for that matter, a thousand symphonies) cannot capture the essence of this thing called womanhood. This is important to consider because our clamoring tries to tame our womanhood, tries to make beauty something attainable rather than something mysterious.

THE PURSUIT OF BEAUTY

Our beauty is beyond our control, but it is our greatest responsibility. The architect Frank Lloyd Wright observed, "If you foolishly ignore beauty, you'll soon find yourself without it. . . . But if you wisely invest in beauty, it will remain with you all the days of your life." But we know—don't we?—how mysterious all that is. We know that women who are most beautiful are intentional about caring for themselves, but we also know their beauty is not manufactured—it just shows up. Lord Byron captured this mystery:

> *And on that cheek, and o'er that brow,*
> *So soft, so calm, yet eloquent,*
> *The smiles that win, the tints that glow,*
> *But tell of days in goodness spent,*
> *A mind at peace with all below,*
> *A heart whose love is innocent!*[1]

Oh, to inspire such words! We get the sense that this woman carries stories and adventures and is content to rest in the mystery of how life has shaped her. Her physical traits carry the beauty of her rich soul. As we read this poem, isn't there something in us that is both jealous to be like her and also sad, almost like he's describing someone too Edenic to exist? That's what beauty is, after all—a whisper of Eden showing up in this cold, stale place.

Before Socrates, before we reasoned ourselves around something as mysterious as creation, beauty was *it*. Beauty and the contemplation of beauty were the focus of existence. For the ancient Greeks, beauty was seen in things without flaw (a perfectly chiseled human form) as *kalos*, and in those who were morally and ethically good as *agathos*.

For the Old Testament Hebrew, beauty could not be separated from a person's personal faith in God. At all times beauty was considered a gift outside one's own control. A lovely little girl or a brilliant young woman or a woman with a delightful manner would all be viewed as women who had been given a tremendous gift that was now their great responsibility before their Maker, the giver of that gift.

Somewhere along the line our responsibility became a pursuit for—no, make that a headlong mission to attain—beauty. This mission even strikes someone such as Helen Gurley Brown (who has clamoring down to a science) as absurd. She tells this story:

> *There was the day my hairpiece fell into the john at the Broadmoor Hotel in Colorado Springs—splash!—just as I was getting ready to put it on and go make a talk to the Magazine Distributors of America. On such an occasion you can either lock yourself in the room and let them send a posse to get you or you can say beauty is absurd and they're going to love me with a flat head.* [2]

We laugh with her, and then she tells us: "Some lovely day perhaps we will all be judged strictly by what we are—not one scrap of attention paid to creamy thighs, goddess cheekbones, Mona Lisa lips, but that isn't the situation now and I'm not sure we, the getting-up-there group, are the ones to strike and demand love and appreciation totally without artifice."[3] She's right, you know. Our culture does its own clamoring—for us to give our hearts away to the pursuit of beauty.

STRUCTURES OF BEAUTY

The structure of the human soul begins to show itself in our choices to either hover or clamor. Teresa of Avila spoke of our hearts being an "interior castle" in which there are literally thousands of rooms that are either sealed off or occupied by the presence of God. Women who have suffered severe abuse often speak of the structures of deceit built up around their hearts to keep them from understanding love. So it is with all of us. As women, our lives take on the foundation, rooms, decor, and landscaping of either trust or fear. The alleyway is where we decide which internal structure we will choose to adorn with our beauty.

These structures are mirrored in the choices made by Israel and Babylon. Israel wandered and forgot her God constantly, but she lived with the promise that God would remember her. No matter how much she turned her back on His kindness, Israel had God's word that He would fight for her, take up for her, speak on her behalf. She had the promise of a constant covering, despite her betrayal, and this covenant unveiled her beauty. The words in Isaiah 54:7-10 reveal the commitment of His vows to her:

"For a brief moment I abandoned you, but with great compassion I will take you back. In a moment of anger I turned my face away for a little while. But with everlasting love I will have compassion on you," says the Lord, your Redeemer.

"Just as I swore in the time of Noah that I would never again let a flood cover the earth and destroy its life, so now I swear that I will never again pour out my anger on you. For the mountains may depart and the hills disappear, but even then I will remain

loyal to you. My covenant of blessing will never be broken," says the Lord, who has mercy on you.

Babylon was not so fortunate. She was mighty, with great prowess to protect herself, but she knew no one was speaking for her—if there was to be a fight, she would have to fight for herself. Babylon knew exactly how to create a beauty for herself. She was a glorious kingdom, full of flash and self-made glory. She was also enamored with her own beauty; she trusted in her lavish richness; she believed she was untouchable. Listen to the severity of God's prediction of what would happen to her:

"Come, Babylon, unconquered one, sit in the dust. For your days of glory, pomp, and honor have ended. O daughter of Babylonia, never again will you be the lovely princess, tender and delicate. Take heavy millstones and grind the corn. Remove your veil and strip off your robe. Expose yourself to public view. You will be naked and burdened with shame. . . .

"You say, 'I'm self-sufficient and not accountable to anyone! I will never be a widow or lose my children.' . . .

"You felt secure in all your wickedness. 'No one sees me,' you said. Your 'wisdom' and 'knowledge' have caused you to turn away from me and claim, 'I am self-sufficient and not accountable to anyone!' So disaster will overtake you suddenly, and you won't be able to charm it away." (Isaiah 47:1–3,8,10–11, emphasis added)

The whispers of Babylon's arrogance and fear can be heard in our hearts whenever we choose the path of clamoring.

THE VOICE OF DRIVENNESS

When we find ourselves in the alleyway and choose clamoring as our response, the voice of drivenness speaks into our ears, *I*

belong in there. . . . I deserve to be in that place of highest privilege.
A cynicism has crept into our culture concerning beauty. We,
along with Babylon, want the place of highest privilege, and we
want it to be something we've created. We have a vague idea of
what it looks like, but it all seems so unattainable. Gene Shalit
once asked Sophia Loren what it was like to be gorgeous. She
said, "I have good friends and, finally, peace of mind," as if she
hadn't heard the question. We salivate to have that kind of centered confidence, don't we?

God wants to unveil our face, showing the beauty in us to
everyone who would see. But we continue our hardened search,
looking for instructions on how to re-create ourselves. As Helen
Gurley Brown says,

> *I was recently chatting with my gorgeous friend Georgette
> Masbacher on the subject of beauty and she said, "The most
> important thing a woman can do if she wants to be beautiful is
> exude a feeling of confidence." I am pounding my forehead.
> "Georgette," I scream. "Where are we getting this confidence if
> we aren't beautiful?" Darling girl didn't know. Beauties are fre-
> quently well meaning on the subject of looks but full of s_ _ _ !
> Great beauties are supposed to suffer more as they age as the
> looks they have so depended on fail. Forget it! We non-great
> beauties suffer just as much.* [4]

Can you hear Babylon's message, that there is a place of highest
privilege for the beautiful, and we must somehow find our way
in and keep ourselves in? It is the oldest lie in the story line:
Satan himself set his sights on the place of highest privilege. The
brilliance he reflected as an angelic being was not enough —
there was more beauty, more glory, to be had. So his attempt to re-
create beauty screamed through the heavens and he was banished
from the very beauty he sought to own. The dilemma is, there
was more beauty. And there is always more beauty for us and
inside of us. But it is not to be owned; it is to be unveiled.

WHAT'S MISSING

Can you hear what's missing in all of this? For the clamoring woman, there is no thought of being one of the masses and no acknowledgment of a common heritage with other women, other sinners. There is no thought that she may be in need of mercy. There is no glance around to others in the alleyway, no living out of the "pure and lasting religion" spoken of in James, that is, caring for orphans and widows (James 1:27).

The place of highest privilege is different for each of us. For one it might be a conversation in which she desires to be the only focus. For another it might be seeking a leadership position for the purpose of having control rather than exercising a loving influence. For another it might be a desire to have her way, no questions asked, in an issue in her marriage. Another may be a prolific Christian leader who constantly speaks in terms of "us" (the godly) and "them" (the world). Each one of these echoes the sentiment "I am, and there is none besides me."

My friend Betsy describes how her heart was given away to this seductive privilege. Because of her own story, she had been living out of an internal message: *I must be the shining star in order to get the love I deserve.* Living from this message caused her to be wracked with jealousy and fear whenever another woman was in the spotlight. As she says, "If someone around me is doing well, shining, it threatens my very survival." Such is the power of this path. We all know what that is like, don't we? One of the most difficult things for us as women is to rejoice with those who rejoice—to let others shine. It is impossible when we are clamoring.

If we cannot own or re-create the beauty inside of us, the only alternative is to allow our true, mysterious, unmanageable beauty—the beauty of a redeemed heart—to be revealed. This is what it means to have an unveiled face (2 Corinthians 3:18). I see an unveiled face when I see a woman weeping for the way she has underestimated her husband. This beauty is seen in a woman who cannot contain her joy over her child's inquisitive questioning of his world. The unveiled face is the countenance of a woman who knows her propensity for rage and has stopped for a minute to plead with God to love through her. Unveiled faces are exposed, vulnerable, and desperate. They reflect God's heart for beauty to be restored and displayed at all costs.

Sharon Hersh speaks of what allows her to have an unveiled face, even in the midst of personal struggle. "I saw more clearly than ever before," she says, "that God became the most hideous creature. . . . I knew in a flash of stunning light, shattering my darkness, that God could look at me with *kamar* (desperate desire) because he had looked away from his own son. This was a God of desperate grace who 'desires all men and women to be saved' (1 Timothy 2:4)."[5]

THE VOICE OF DETERMINATION

Along with drivenness, determination lies along the path of clamoring. It says, *I'll become what they want. I'll re-create myself into what they are looking for. I will charm my way in.*

We all do it—try to re-create ourselves. We do it in the obvious ways, seen in the magazines lining the grocery store's checkout aisle as well as in the most devoted Gold's Gym goddesses. But re-creating ourselves takes on more subtle forms when it is internal, not merely makeup, diets, and silicone. We re-create ourselves when we determine to become someone other than our true self. We try to charm away the prospect of bearing our desire and feeling our loneliness. We survey the relationship and the situation and determine what it is our friend, spouse, church, boss, or family member is looking for, and we give it to them. This is not merely codependency; it is a deep fear that our true self is unlovely, unwanted, and forgotten.

Claire spent fifteen years of marriage consumed with the mission of re-creating herself. What she created was quite impressive.

She was married to a successful businessman who was an elder at a prominent church. She became the right-hand woman of a popular Bible teacher, traveling with her and doing teaching herself, always concerned (as she should have been) with handling the Word carefully and being disciplined in memorization and study. She could make your head spin with her knowledge. And she asked of others the same level of mastery.

The problem was, Claire is an artist. She's a philosopher, a poet. She came from a chaotic home, full of torment. She encountered evil daily in her home as a child. Her heart was filled with philosopher's questions, artist's images, and the poetry born in pain. But somewhere in her alleyway she determined that such impassioned questions are useless, don't change things anyway, and certainly never got her back into the restaurant. So Claire looked around. It was a religious world she was in, so she'd become really, really good at it. She became what she thought "they" wanted—at least she'd have a place at *some* table that way. She re-created herself and lost herself, and therefore lost God's glory in the process.

Was her frenzied pursuit of biblical knowledge a complete waste? Hardly. Things have changed a bit, and Claire is living out her knowledge from a deeper place of trust that God sees her, knows her, and is concerned about her alleyway. She has a deeper sense of who she is waiting for, so her knowledge of Him has a pulse rather than an outline. Slowly God is meeting her in her desire rather than being held at bay by all her "understanding" of Him. Slowly her artistry is coming back.

NOTHING NEW

Women have been trying to re-create themselves throughout history—it's like a sport to us. A competition with other women, in the company of other women. It's a sport that goes far beyond tuning up physically or coming up with a new persona. We want to win. Both the Lord and Babylon claim, "I am . . . , and there is no other" (Isaiah 45:18; see Isaiah 47:10, NIV). The goal of our sport is to be worshiped. The problem is, this sport has made us weary. We want to ascend to goddesslike beauty without being reconciled with the Creator who breathed beauty into us. So we try to create our own external beauty and at the same time stay centered and flowing with internal beauty. It can't be done.

Women from conservative worlds and feminists alike occasionally realize this sport is getting us nowhere. Journalist and feminist Naomi Wolf admits, "Just as the beauty myth did not really care what women looked like as long as women felt ugly, we must see that it does not matter in the least what women look like as long as we feel beautiful." She goes on to say,

> The problem with cosmetics exists only when women feel invisible or inadequate without them. The problem with working out exists only if women hate ourselves when we don't. When a woman is forced to adorn herself to buy a hearing, when she needs her grooming in order to protect her identity, when she goes hungry in order to keep her job, when she must attract a lover so that she can take care of her children, that is exactly what makes "beauty" hurt.[6]

Our determination to create our own beauty *does* hurt. It is an affront to God's heart. He desires to simply release us — to unveil us — to be beautiful. Isn't that what the garden was? It was God's releasing of Eve to be as beautiful as she really was. Karen Lee-Thorpe and Cynthia Hicks say this about Eve and the seed of our frenzied pursuit of re-creation: In Eden, before her sin, Eve must have radiated the glory of God's image from her soul and spirit out through her body. Her body, untainted by aging or disease, would have been the perfect form Adam's flesh was designed to seek. She would have been a woman that we, if we saw her, would be tempted to call a goddess. But she and her husband followed Satan in believing their almost-divine glory entitled them to set themselves up as actual god and goddess

of their world. Ezekiel's words about the king of Tyre could
apply to all three of them:

> Your heart became proud
> on account of your beauty,
> And you corrupted your wisdom
> because of your splendor.[7]

The seed of corrupted beauty, again, is found in the desire to
own it, to have mastery over it. Our hearts are beautiful in the
alleyway only when we stop clamoring long enough to let desire
have its way with us.

THE VOICE OF CLAMORING FEAR

Our vulnerability begins to be heard in the voice of fear: *I'll
keep myself busy so I'm not discovered as a fraud.*

A few years ago a good friend and I were at a luncheon. She
pointed out the wife of a mutual friend seated at another table.
This woman was radiant, at rest. And to top it off, she had a
simple, luminous diamond necklace draped around her neck,
hanging delicately over her gorgeous clavicle bones. My friend
whispered, "Now there's a well-loved woman!" So true. There is a
lavish quality to a woman who knows she is spoken for, committed to, well loved. Her richness does not come from any jewels,
but the jewels suit her because she has an internal sense of royalty.

Babylon had a manufactured sense of royalty. She determined
to adorn herself with manufactured jewels. Israel had beauty that
came from one place only: remembering the promise of the covenant and the truth that God would fight for her in spite of herself.
The jewels she wears fit her because she was made for them.

Here our fear is exposed. We are convinced that we've been
ushered out of that restaurant because of infirmities and imper-
fections in ourselves—we didn't have the right jewels. We knew
it all along, and we feel ridiculous for having relaxed and
enjoyed ourselves. Who were we kidding? Now the aim is clear:

make sure none of those weaknesses show up again so as to disqualify us from being let back in.

You would never know that Babylon was afraid — she appeared so strong. But Babylon had the fear most central to a feminine soul, the fear of being unlovely and being forgotten. Babylon was constantly working on her appearance so that her name would not be forgotten. We're Babylon when we are looking for our own name. In our fear that no one will speak on our behalf or protect us or fight for us, we start to re-create both ourselves and our role in the story. We manipulate our surroundings so we don't feel so defenseless. We never look outside ourselves for the answer — we are certain the answer lies within our capacity to come up with some change, some way to get us back into the restaurant. Some way to please those in our lives who can either feed our hearts or abruptly disappoint us.

What we don't realize in our clamoring is that we are already spoken for. Isaiah 54 is a picture of expansiveness, lavishness, restoration, and finery, all of which are entirely the result of God's covenant to Israel, which He will not revoke, no matter how tempted He is. He says this to His betrothed, Jerusalem:

"O storm–battered city, troubled and desolate! I will rebuild you on a foundation of sapphires and make the walls of your houses from precious jewels. I will make your towers of sparkling rubies and your gates and walls of shining gems. I will teach all your citizens, and their prosperity will be great. You will live under a government that is just and fair. Your enemies will stay far away; you will live in peace. Terror will not come near. If any nation comes to fight you, it will not be because I sent them to punish you. Your enemies will always be defeated because I am on your side." (Isaiah 54:11–15)

Israel becomes more tender, delicate, and lovely; Babylon becomes more parched, desperate, and barren. Israel and Babylon shared the same forgetfulness — neither of them was seeking God nor remembering His goodness. But Israel had the promise that she would not be forgotten.

We *are* spoken for. First Peter 1:3-9 says we are called to a living hope that is found in the death, burial, and resurrection of Christ. Our heritage flows from our love affair with the One who has spoken for us. The fruit of our love affair is our beauty; it is not something we can manufacture, manipulate, or control. Beauty springs entirely from the One who lavishes jewels and finery within our hearts. He sees our clamoring, hears our rage, knows our fear, and yet He runs to us to lift the veil from our face with His bloodstained hands. We are beautiful to Him.

4

THE FOOLISH
PATH OF HOPE

Great spirits have always encountered
violent opposition from mediocre minds.
—ALBERT EINSTEIN

Where there is no vision, the people perish.
—KING SOLOMON

Just because someone can't
see doesn't mean he has no vision.
—STEVIE WONDER

When a woman finds herself thrown out of the Restaurant of
Hope, abandoned to the cold, dark alleyway, she can pursue the
path of hovering. Hunkering down over the steam grate, she can
lower her expectations to the basement and try to be satisfied
with merely surviving. Or she can pursue the path of clamoring,
trying in her own strength to make herself beautiful enough to

be invited back into the restaurant. This pathway is a dead end like the other. But there's a third pathway. The final option in the alleyway is an option that feels foolish—the option of hopeful remembrance and vision. Frederick Buechner says, "The world can be kind, and it can be cruel. It can be beautiful, and it can be appalling. It can give us good reason to hope and good reason to give up all hope. It can strengthen our faith in a loving God, and it can decimate our faith."[1] The alleyway makes this clear.

Choosing to respond to hope requires courage, vision, and patience. The third path looks something like this: *How sad. How very sad. I've been ushered away from the meal I know the chef intended for me. As I look around this alleyway, everything I see is cold, dark, and lonely. I'm going to slowly look around the harshness of this place, and then I will weep. I will weep for what has been lost. Then I will set my gaze through that back kitchen window. From just the right angle, I'm able to see the table where I once sat. As the back door opens and closes, the aromas of the kitchen hit my senses and remind me of what I had. I will not cover my eyes; I will not cover my nose. I will allow myself to be reminded of what was. And I will wait. I will not wait merely for the meal to be restored to me—that may never happen. But I will wait for God. It is His gaze, His care for me that haunts me, and it is His seeming abandonment that puzzles me. In the waiting I will wrestle with my own personal dilemma with the chef. And in the waiting I will offer my presence to those around me; I will find opportunities to love.*

WHAT HOPE LOOKS LIKE

At first glance, hope seems a lofty-minded friend, attempting to call us away from all that is realistic and practical in life. But as we become better acquainted with hope's ways, we see that the contrary is true—it is a call to enter reality. Look for the courage, vision, and patience in these snapshots:

∽ *A four-year-old child daily anticipating his June birthday*
. . . in February

∽ *An eighty-seven-year-old woman praying quietly for God to*
allow her to come home

∽ *A woman choosing to shed tender tears with her husband*
(not just in front of him), knowing he has told her how
uncomfortable tears make him

∽ *A man in a stale marriage, choosing to initiate physical*
intimacy with his wife when she has rebuffed such advances
in the past

∽ *A single woman investing heart and soul in the lives of both*
single and married friends

These snapshots reveal a glimpse of what hope looks like.
Can you see how each person could be indicted as "foolish"?
Can you see the courage required to enter reality? Each person
was envisioning something that wasn't there yet. If you have
something already, you don't need to hope for it (Romans 8:24).
And can you see how hoping causes us to love in ways that
would not be possible without a vision of what might be? Love
bears all things, hopes all things, believes all things, endures all
things (1 Corinthians 13:7).

The little boy envisioning his birthday cake knows a winsome
freedom that doesn't require much of him. He has his vision,
and it brings him instant delight! The eighty-seven-year-old
woman certainly has a vision too, and she longs for release. Her
vision brings her comfort in the midst of physical suffering. The
anticipation of hope is always life-giving.

The woman weeping with her husband has a vision. This
requires more of her than what she is hoping for in him. She
has a hope that her husband might not flee in the midst of her

sadness, that he would be present with her, a strong companion. As she offers tears without demanding he respond perfectly, she wears hope's garments — tenderness, strength, and honor. Waiting in hope is never without honor.

A man in a stale marriage, who grants his wife the opportunity to respond to him. He honors her by not giving up in spite of past rejection. He honors himself by reflecting God's heart, pursuing her even in the face of apparent disinterest.

The single person's investment in life can be heard in many tones — monotone, minor key, and symphonic. Monotone singles have pushed aside their dreams and longings and have thrown themselves into a frenetic pursuit of anything to keep their heart at bay. Minor-key singles seem to have entered their longings, never to return. Their lives have a tone of constant melancholy. Singleness in the minor key is a state of shame. A single person investing heart and soul in the lives of friends, whether married or single, is a symphony. She lives from a posture of admitting her deep thirst for companionship and marriage. There are occasional minor chords because she can look at her life and know that singleness was not God's original intent. These minor chords are mingled with grand major chords, perfectly timed crescendos, and rests, all coming from the ebb and flow of God's work in her life. The music of hope is slightly unsettling.

Hope's anticipation, waiting, movement, and music all flow from vision.

VISION'S STRENGTH

Vision came to me in the form of a puppy. Salvation wrapped in a little black face and brown paws. I went to a tiny high-country store to buy some bread and fill my car with gas. There she sat on the store's cement stoop, quite sleepy when we met. Her brothers and sister — eight in all, I believe — were strewn around the porch on laps, in boxes, held by little kids. I knew immediately from the look in the eye of the woman attending to this little parade of canines that she meant business—these puppies were being given away.

One puppy was a bright-eyed wonder, all black except for a brown stripe running horizontally across her breast. With big, broad paws on a tiny puppy body, she stole my heart. *I must be crazy,* I thought. But that thought wasn't strong enough to push down the sheer desire to love her. Against my better judgment, I scooped her up and said, "I'll take this one." That afternoon I decided to name her Vallecito Corazon; Vallecito Lake was home to both of us and *corazón* means "heart" in Spanish. God loved her enough to stripe her heart. *I can relate, puppy,* I thought. I'd call her Cito.

How a creature could pour strength into my veins in just a few days of sharing life with me, I do not know. But Cito succeeded in doing just that. I was dreading this trip, you see. I wasn't sure how my weary heart could bear being surrounded by the beauty I've loved since a child, without my sharing it with someone. I was to have shared this trip with the man I was going to marry. This trip was happening shortly before the date that was to have been our wedding day. He was not here. There would be no wedding. And though my heart was gaining strength, my bewildered soul wasn't sure how to handle being in this sacred space, in this stunning beauty, without him.

So, a puppy made a difference? Pretty absurd thought. Buechner says we are in constant danger of being reactors in the drama of our lives rather than actors. He goes on to say, "In our lives in the world, the temptation is always to go where the world takes us, to drift with whatever current happens to be running strongest. When good things happen, we rise to heaven; when bad things happen, we descend to hell. When the world strikes out at us, we strike back, and when one way or another the world blesses us, our spirits soar."[2] Cito kept me from drowning in the strong current of heartache. Crazy, isn't it? A puppy? Her canine needs have been an unknowing lifeline to what disappointment, shame, and rejection have sought to sweep away. She laughs at my foolish ways. She really doesn't care how well I think or write or counsel or ski. She just likes trotting along behind me, slightly crooked, down a rocky mountain path. If I talk out loud while walking or stop and weep a little, she doesn't care. She has brought perspective, but far more, she has invited me to new vision.

Notice I say "invited." As wonderful as this little dog is, she doesn't quite cut it. Craig Barnes says, "We have adjusted to the harshness of life. We have learned that as long as life isn't tragic we can tolerate the fact that it will be vaguely dissatisfying. But nowhere in Scripture does hope appear for those who have learned to cope by settling for a little glory."[3] I don't want to ever settle for the sort of mundane happiness Cito brings me.

New Eyes

Perspective. It is the thing that stocks the self-help section of bookstores. As women, especially, we are frantic for ways of coping. We buy books to gain perspective on attention deficits, divorce and remarriage, diet and exercise, how to be a godly woman. *Perspective* is a keyword in our society. But doesn't it leave you flat? The *American Heritage Dictionary* includes in its definitions of *perspective* this wording: "Subjective evaluation of relative significance; point of view." Is a new point of view what produces change when our hearts are swept away in disappointment and we are looking for some moorings? In many ways, yes. But perspective settles for a little glory. God does not have perspective about our transformation; He *sees* it. Perspective shifts the puzzle pieces of our circumstances around until we feel better about the picture; vision sees what the puzzle was meant to be.

Perspective helps us cope, but coping is so much less than what our lives were made for. I can't imagine Jesus looking around at His twelve friends at the Last Supper and saying,

"You can have the peace I leave with you if you work really hard at keeping a good perspective on things." No, He invites them to see differently, to see beyond. He says, "My peace I give you. I do not give to you as the world gives. Do not let your hearts be troubled and do not be afraid" (John 14:27, NIV). Jesus tells us there is something different that we haven't seen yet—what we need are new eyes. Perspective must flow from a vision for more, for what we haven't yet seen, or it becomes just another self-help frame of mind. Macrina Wiederkehr points us to these words from *The Cloud of Unknowing:* "It is not what you are nor what you have been that God sees with his all merciful eyes, but what you desire to be."[4] My puppy reminded me of what I've lost, what I long for, and the simple fact that there is more to life than just my loss. She's invited me to vision without even knowing it. The same dictionary defines *vision* as "the manner in which one sees or perceives of something" and as "a mental image produced by the imagination."

The manner in which one sees. The apostle Paul was not out-lining a new perspective when he said the following words to the fledgling church in Ephesus. He couldn't settle for a little glory because he loved his friends. He saw them through new eyes, and this is what came from his heart as a result:

I have never stopped thanking God for you. I pray for you constantly, asking God, the glorious Father of our Lord Jesus Christ, to give you spiritual wisdom and understanding, so that you might grow in your knowledge of God. I pray that your hearts will be flooded with light so that you can understand the wonderful future he has promised to those he called. I want you to realize what a rich and glorious inheritance he has given to his people.

I pray that you will begin to understand the incredible greatness of his power for us who believe him. This is the same mighty power that raised Christ from the dead and seated him in the place of honor at God's right hand in the heavenly realms. (Ephesians 1:16–22)

How would words like this go over at an Anthony Robbins seminar? Or at the last committee meeting you went to, for that matter? Can you hear how vision is not cheerleading ourselves into something more? Vision is imaginative and filled with desire, and it is desperate because it knows its lack. Where does such passionate vision come from? I believe our sense of imagination grows as we see that we are not the only ones. As we bump into other people, we get glimpses of the beauty God intended for us. C. S. Lewis said, "Ah, but we want so much more. . . . We do not want merely to see beauty, though, God knows, even that is bounty enough. We want something else which can hardly be put into words—to be united with the beauty we see, to pass into it, to receive it into ourselves, to bathe in it, to become part of it."5

John Powell says that our vision is not merely dreaming or conjuring up something we want, but it is in fact *metanoia,* or a change of vision. In Greek culture this meant a literal change in outlook or a complete change of thinking. Powell writes, "I once thought the disciples were slow, but not now. I now think that the real challenge of Jesus was not a matter of intelligence but ultimately a challenge to give up an old vision and to accept a new one."6 We have to be desperate for that to happen. Dallas Willard says this is what we truly want. "The repentance in which we pine for our life and world to really be different, the authentic *metanoia* which Christ opens us to in His gospel, comes upon us as we are given a vision of the majesty, holiness, and goodness of God."7

As we start to see with new eyes, we realize that the world has continued, that we really are okay, even though the suffering is great. Buechner puts it this way: "It is in Jesus, of course, and in the people whose lives have been deeply touched by Jesus, and in ourselves at those moments when we also are deeply touched by him, that we see another way of being human in this world, which is the way of wholeness."8 This is what my heroes have done for me. When our stolen dreams are the only ones in front of our eyes, there is no choice but for us to lose heart. When our vision is expanded to include prostitutes turned tender, crusty women turned luminous, lonely women turned lavish, we find that our dreams matter to God.

VISION AND THE FUTURE

Perspective helps put my feet on the path. Vision keeps me going regardless of how long the path is, and it allows beauty to intrude in surprising ways. For some, Solomon's words that we perish without vision (Proverbs 29:18, KJV) are literal. On a recent trip to Poland, a dear friend took me to Auschwitz, which is a macabre twenty-minute drive from her village. The cloud of evil rests thickly over the block buildings and clay grounds.

There are no words for what this place did to me in two hours. How a human could bear existence there for six months or two years, I could not take in. As I walked into building after building of evidence—viewing hundreds of yards of human hair (kept to make fabric), shoes, baby clothes, glasses—I couldn't find my heart. I had to disconnect from the truth of it to make it through the tour. And then we came into a hallway with photographs. For whatever taunting reason—who knows evil's reasoning?—the Nazis had taken before and after shots of many brought into the camp. It was those pictures that let me look individuals in the eye. Suddenly it was *this* man's lock of hair, *this* woman's glasses, *her* baby's clothes. Suddenly I could no longer disconnect. I was overcome with sorrow and rage.

And then we entered the building notorious for being the deepest place of cruelty. No question, the gas chamber was preferable to this place. Human beings made to stand upright, pressed against each other, in concrete rooms each no larger than a small closet. They were made to stand till their death, enduring untold torture and mockery. In this hell, in the darkest corner, a small spotlight shines on a word etched into the cold, damp wall: "Jesus." Some person, snatched away from family and friends through trickery and fraud, who lived out her (or his) last days in the company of demons, had taken what feeble strength was left in her emaciated body to envision her only strength and future. And her future was Jesus. The beauty (and perhaps mystery) of His name kept someone, on the road to death, alive for another moment.

Jesus finds His way in. He reintroduces the vision we want so much to kill. He gently says, "Remember Me." He is unobtrusive but impossible to ignore. Evil rages, and He gently whispers. Jesus doesn't give us lessons on perspective; He compels us to see.

THE SENSUALITY OF QUESTIONS

The gospel's invitation is not quite what we might think—it is not an invitation to rise above our senses. Instead, it goes like this: "Look around at the cold, hard concrete in the alley. Feel the sting of winter's chill. Smell the lingering aroma of the fine meal. Relax long enough to be touched by how bad things are and how stunning beauty is. Stop long enough to dream of the feast to come. And as you are awakened, please realize that you have many questions of God." C. S. Lewis said, "All the leaves of the New Testament are rustling with the rumour that it will not always be so. Some day, God willing, we shall get in."[9] Kathleen Norris says, "When God-talk is speech that is not of this world, it is a false language. In a religion that celebrates the Incarnation—the joining together of the human and the divine—a spiritualized jargon that does not ground itself in the five senses should be anathema."[10] Our senses bring us to the place Meister Eckhart knew when he said, "God is like a person who clears his throat while hiding and so gives himself away." Sometimes we can't find God in the alleyway, but our senses tell us He's been there. And these senses take us into the deepest questions of our heart.

In order for a woman to be a visionary, she must first be willing to face what is not there—in herself, in those she loves, in her circumstances, in her world. Remember, the alleyway makes us face our dilemma with God. It is here that the questions already inside us surface. They are not new questions; they are simply questions we become adept at fleeing through our hovering, our clamoring, our simple forgetfulness. The words of Henri Nouwen apply here: "To offer answers before there are questions is equal to spiritual oppression." We offer ourselves answers before we've really faced our questions, so we are oppressive with our own hearts. The alleyway asks us to see what is gone, what has been taken, what is missing. You cannot have a vision for something unless that something is missing. Again, the apostle Paul told us that if we already have something, we don't need to hope for it (Romans 8:24). C. S. Lewis said, "At present we are on the outside of the world, the wrong side of the door. We discern the freshness and purity of morning, but they do not make us fresh and pure."[11] If we allow our senses to be stirred and then face our heart's questions, we can be released from the oppressive ways we live.

I can still see her face as she said, "That's in the *Bible?*" My client was stunned as I read to her from Psalm 88. This psalm is one long discourse on how God had let the psalmist down. Some of the psalm's choicest complaints are these: "You have caused my friends to loathe me; you have sent them all away. I am in a trap with no way of escape. My eyes are blinded by my tears" (verses 8-9). And, "Your fierce anger has overwhelmed me. Your terrors have cut me off. They swirl around me like floodwaters all day long" (verses 16-17). Then the psalm *ends* by saying, "You have taken away my companions and loved ones; only darkness remains" (verse 18).

My client never knew God invites such discourse. These words filled her heart, but she never had permission to take them to God. She didn't know He would rather have us railing, with face turned toward Him, than have us feign contentment as we turn our face from Him in our sullen anger. Why? Because He wants to see us rage? No, it is because He already knows we're furious, and it is our fury, after all, that He died for. Dan Allender says, "For many, strong feelings are an infrequent, foreign experience. Their inner life is characterized by an inner coolness, bordering on indifference. Unfortunately, this is often mistaken for trust."[12]

Can you see how, for women, this is often mistaken for the "gentle and quiet spirit, which is so precious to God" (1 Peter 3:4)? We've somehow created an image of godliness that is closer to pablum than it is to salt and light. Again, we want to jump over the desperation and loneliness of the Fall and land in a place of serene contentment. The only way to achieve that is through the "religion of tips and principles" spoken of in *The Sacred Romance*. But God wants our hearts. Allender continues:

> *In many circles, passionate emotions are discouraged as unspiritual. You are considered godly if you can handle difficult trials with a detached and apparently unruffled confidence. But this conclusion is wrong. There are times when lack of emotion is simply the byproduct of hardness and arrogance. The Scriptures reveal that this absence of feeling is often a refusal to face the sorrow of life and the hunger for heaven; it is not the mark of maturity, but rather the boast of evil.*[13]

Only when we move through the questions do we realize our need for God's comfort in our loneliness, and our need for forgiveness for our determined attempts at control. Standing in the alleyway, clenching our teeth, closing our eyes, and proclaiming a silent mantra—"I am loved, I am loved, I am not forgotten"—is hardly the route to vision. If anything, it is the route to greater disillusion and discouragement.

I don't know if you've discovered it yet, but repetitive choruses cannot change our heart's questions. Our humble God comes face to face with us as we're midsentence in telling Him what a lousy job He's doing with our lives. There He reveals His face, which doesn't rage but rather says, "Want to feast?" This brings us to a place where we can say the words of Psalm 73:21-26 without pretending, because we have seen how much confusion, rage, and anger is in our hearts:

> *Then I realized how bitter I had become,*
> *how pained I had been by all I had seen.*
> *I was so foolish and arrogant,*
> *I must have seemed like a senseless animal to you.*
> *Yet I still belong to you;*
> *you are holding my right hand.*
> *You will keep on guiding me with your counsel,*
> *leading me to a glorious destiny.*
> *Whom have I in heaven but you?*
> *I desire you more than anything on earth.*
> *My health may fail, and my spirit may grow weak.*
> *but God remains the strength of my heart;*
> *he is mine forever.*

WHEN VISION MEETS REALITY

"To truly love someone is to see them as God intended," said Fyodor Dostoyevsky.[14] These are fighting words more than words of unconditional love. The vision of a good friend unravels us. Thomas Merton said this:

> *If we are to love sincerely, and with simplicity, we must first of all overcome the fear of not being loved. And this cannot be done by forcing ourselves to believe in some illusion, saying that we are loved when we are not. We must first strip ourselves of our greatest illusions about ourselves, frankly recognize in how many ways we are unlovable, descend into the depths of our being until we come to the basic reality that is in us, and learn to see that we are loveable after all, in spite of everything!*[15]

A good friend pulled that hanging thread in my life recently. Prior to her tug, I had been in a rut but just kept moving. We were together on behalf of a mutual friend who was headed off in a new direction. The entire visit, I was flighty and preoccupied. My friend was horrified by my selfish preoccupations, in which I steered conversations back to myself with finesse. She was horrified, she explained later, not only because it took away from our visit and celebration of our mutual friend's life, but because she knows me and she couldn't see me.

As she shared this with me, I was sorrowful over my selfishness and grateful that someone cared enough to seek me out. As I felt the tug on the thread from which I was hanging, I felt the sweet power of brokenness overtake me. Not because I sought it out but because my friend sought it out for me and in me. This is where the rubber of vision—allowing ourselves to see clearly who someone can become—meets the road of reality.

As my friend gave me this sweet but painful gift, I was reminded of Godric, the eccentric saint of whom Buechner writes in his novel by the same name. As Godric tells the story of his life, he asks the question "What is friendship, when all's said and done, but the giving and taking of wounds?"[16] Vision always propels us into deeper levels of relationship.

PRESENCE VERSUS BARRENNESS

There was a sigh in the heart of the friend I just mentioned. No disgust, no condemnation, just a deep sigh as she looked at me in light of the vision she has for me. How do *you* sigh? In the midst of your dearest relationships, when the shoulders go up, the lungs fill, and the release of air and emotion comes, what kind of release is it for you? Is it a release of disgust? Is it a sigh you might hear on the heating vent in the alleyway, an I-should-have-known-you-would-disappoint-me kind of resignation? Is it a clamoring sigh, proclaiming disgust with every pound on the door, a sigh of disapproval of how you are being handled? Or is it a sigh that says, "Ouch! I do believe another contraction is setting in. I hope for so much for you and, yes, *from* you. I feel so disappointed at this moment, but I'm reminded that giving birth is filled with anticipation and agony."

Think of two or three people in your life, people who are fixtures—always there. Now ask yourself whether they offer you their presence, meaning you can walk away from the simplest interaction with them and feel slightly unnerved, challenged. You cannot walk away from them unchanged. Now think of people who offer a barrenness of soul, meaning you could hang out with them for great lengths of time and never really have to change or consider the way you are living. Their life provokes nothing more. The barren people are those Eugene Peterson speaks of as those who are easily observed but never encountered.[17] Now ask yourself, in which category would your friends place you?

Susan was a woman with whom I met for counseling years ago. We met for a catch-up cup of coffee recently and were reminiscing about the presence that had grown in her life as a result of responding to the hope within her. She was luminous. It was a nice change. Barrenness characterized her when we first met. I'll never forget those initial days—she was one of the nicest people to observe, but I continually found myself thinking, *Where is the rest of you?* Susan's husband, at the time, was addicted to cocaine. It was a common occurrence for him to stay out until 4:00 A.M., stumble home, grab a bagel, and kiss her on the cheek as he wandered out the door to work. As I listened to these stories, what hung in the air for me were the words Susan chose. She kept using words like "irritating," "frustrating," "confusing." I was thinking words like "furious," "betrayed," "terrified." It didn't take long, as I painted simple pictures of what she legitimately longed for and needed, for her to realize that she was indeed furious, betrayed, and terrified. Was the goal of this exercise for Susan to "get in touch with her pain"? Certainly that was part of the process, but only a small part of becoming a woman to be encountered, a woman with presence.

Susan had tamed her words, you see. We all do it. We make our hearts vague and uninteresting. We try to take the sting out of the arrows. As we bridle the truth of our disappointments and tone down the words we use to tell our stories, we convince ourselves we can make it. But that's not hope; that's conjured and fake perseverance. It doesn't last long. Eventually, if we have integrity, we become tired of such ridiculous façades and admit all is not well.

This admission is imperative if we are to respond to hope's vision. Susan allowed herself to weep over her situation, and she allowed her vision to become one of offering herself to her husband in courageous and subversive ways. She became a woman who wept in front of her husband, displaying to him the horrendous damage he was doing. She finally respected him enough to challenge his foolishness for the first time in their married life. What a gamble! Live without vision and you can ease into the flow of life seemingly unscathed. Respond to hope and you will weep. You will also offer a haunting fragrance of the gospel, often to those who want no part in it.

COURAGE TO ENVISION THE OUTSIDE

Several years ago I was haunted by scenes from the movie *The Shawshank Redemption*. In it, Andy Dufresne (Tim Robbins) is sentenced to life in Shawshank Maximum Security Prison for killing his wife. An unlikely candidate for incarceration, Andy is befriended by Red (Morgan Freeman), and the two of them live out the hours of untold horror, violence, and sexual degradation found in prison.

Two scenes linger in my memory. In the first, an elderly inmate, Brooks, receives his parole after fifty years behind the walls of Shawshank. Inside, Brooks had become a soft-spoken, kind, and perceptive man who administered the prison library with care (and delivered contraband into the prison with finesse). But he had lived with no vision for the outside.

Released to a freedom he neither desires nor can handle, Brooks lasts only two weeks before the pressure becomes too great and he takes his own life in the lonely halfway house that was his new home. When Andy and Red receive news of Brooks's death, Red's reply is "These walls are funny. First you hate 'em. Then you get used to 'em. Enough time passes, you get so you depend on 'em. That's institutionalized."

Unlike Brooks, Andy has a perpetual vision of the outside that his friends mock. A few weeks after Brooks's suicide, Andy receives word that his constant requests for materials to update the library have been granted. Boxes of books, an old phonograph, and a selection of records arrive with Andy's name on them. Andy seizes the moment, and in a scene where time stands still, he hooks the phonograph up to the prison sound system. Soon the voices of two opera divas singing a Mozart aria pour into the prison yard. One by one the inmates stop their movement. They are captured, seized by the oddity of the music's beauty and its intrusion into their sad existence. Each prisoner becomes caught up in a penetrating reminder of the outside. They cannot run. The music causes them to be free.

Andy spends several weeks in "the hole" for his stunt, but he proclaims to his friends afterward, "It was the easiest time I ever did." When the other prisoners question this, he explains that nobody could take it from him, that music. He wonders if anyone knew what he meant. He is met only with blank stares. "It's what is in here [touching his heart]. It is hope."

Red becomes indignant. "Hope? Andy, hope is a dangerous thing. Hope can make you crazy. If you are smart, you'll just forget about hope."

Andy knowingly asks, "Just the way Brooks did?"

When we kill our vision for what was intended for us, we become like Brooks. We commit soul suicide, barely bearing up under life "inside the walls," not able to fully drink in tastes of the "outside." Andy lived with a specific vision of where he would go if he were released. It was a sunny beach in Mexico.

That vision did make him crazy at times, but it also made him the man who revolutionized an entire prison.

So, how does all this impact the heart of a woman? Women who impact others with their presence are those who see with new eyes, whether in a prison, on a long walk in the park, during an afternoon at the office, while dealing with the loss of a baby, or when confronting a husband's addiction. They know what Buechner knows:

> Whatever they think I may have in the way of comfort and healing, and I, who in the old days would have shrunk with fear from any such charged encounter, try to find something wise and hopeful to say to them, only little by little coming to understand that the most precious thing I have to give them is not whatever words I find to say—but simply whatever, spoken or unspoken, I have in me of Christ, which is also the most precious thing they have to give me. All too rarely, I regret to say, my search has taken me also to a sacred and profoundly silent place inside myself, where it is less that I pray than that, to paraphrase Saint Paul, the Holy Spirit, I believe, prays within me and for me with sighs too deep for words. (Romans 8:26).[18]

5

BOREDOM AND BREAD

She's tryin' to be a good girl and give 'em
what they want, but Margery's dreaming of horses.
— COUNTING CROWS

In the light to free me from my burden and bring
me life eternally . . . I have created my own prison.
— CREED

My heart calls to me in my sleep — how can
I turn to it 'cause I'm all locked up in this Dark Place.
— DAVE MATTHEWS BAND

Let's face it. Without vision, the alleyway is boring. Little to stir our hearts. Boredom is one of the greatest enemies of the female heart, but we actually seek it out in our addictions. Our hovering and clamoring reveal that we prefer boredom (dulling our senses) to desire.

"Bored? How can I possibly be bored?" you might ask. Our lives are so packed with schedule items and stimulus, it's hard to imagine that this life, even when jolted with interruptions, can be boring. We may feel burned out and haggard, but surely we aren't bored. Helen Keller said, "Life is either a daring adventure or nothing." Somehow I don't think she had shopping, marijuana, or emotional affairs in mind when she envisioned a daring adventure. So hang with me here. Life is not boring—we *make* it boring. Let me explain.

Think back for a moment to the daydreaming little girl. She was still, but not bored. Her mind and heart were a fertile playground of imagination. As she dreamed, she allowed her longing and desire to stimulate her. She was still and stirred up (to anticipation) at the same time. Now picture her mindlessly rattling away on an arcade video game. See what happens? Now she is moving and receiving constant stimuli, but her soul is not being awakened. We make our minds and hearts bored by filling them with things that don't stimulate our desire. Oh, these things stimulate our bodies and minds, our fantasies and pulses, but they do not stimulate our desire.

The boring alleyway is the perfect place for getting fat, having an affair, getting more parts of your body pierced, getting skinny, trying cocaine or ecstasy, maxing out a credit card, pouring yourself more devotedly into your schedule of ministry, devouring some romance novels, developing some great networks of gossip, drowning yourself in an addictive and dependent relationship, discovering pornography Web sites. Why? Because there's nothing else to do? No, because we are running from desire. C. S. Lewis said the problem with most Christians is that they don't want enough. Again, how can that be? How can it be that I want too little when I feel wanton and frivolous for wanting the things I do want? But if we are honest, we can easily see the truth in Lewis's familiar words: "We are half-hearted creatures, fooling about with drink and sex and ambition when infinite joy is offered us, like an ignorant child who wants to go on making mud pies in a slum because he cannot imagine what is meant by the offer of a holiday at the sea. We are far too easily pleased."[1]

My closet is obscene. Since I was a teenager, it has been a picture of my tendencies toward excess. I could probably clothe a small country in Asia with the multiple shirts, sweaters, and shoes. So, my problem is one of not wanting enough? Sounds backward, doesn't it? Stay with me as we continue to see how our desire gets stunted and turned upside down.

It's not likely that the picture you have of your fine meal includes mass quantities of peanut butter cups. That's like fantasizing about having an affair with Pee Wee Herman when we could have a romance with Mel Gibson. Surely our imagination has more finesse than this. So, why do we run headlong into the boredom of such indulgence? Why is it that dulling ourselves in the boredom of a bag of chips or TV seems so much more bearable than an exquisite French meal, with its subtle aromas, or a fiery New Mexican meal, rich with texture and bite?

MANNA AND MAGGOTS

It's not a new phenomenon. The Israelites had manna—flaky honey cakes covering the ground every morning—and it was boring. The same every day. But it was manna *from heaven*. It was designed to be just enough. The honey-cake diet called them to remember God and to trust in His care and provision. It was meant to cause them to hunger for what was coming down the road in a place called Canaan. We are so forgetful, you see. We can barely remember what's on our grocery list, let alone remember the God of the universe. Without His everyday manna (reminders) in our lives, and without our hearts gathering it in, we simply forget where we are headed and who is taking us there. We forget what we are hungry for.

Down the road was a place flowing with milk *and* honey—a place of lavish pleasure, great beauty, and fulfilling work—not just honey cakes. Here was a taste; coming was the real deal, the real meal. Our manna intrudes into our hours on the freeway and into our frenzied pace. A translucent flower, a handmade tapestry, a photograph of a child, a pot of homemade stew on a snowy night, a quiet time of prayer, jolting lyrics, an extravagant and sensual wedding party—these are our honey cakes. The real deal is coming.

When the Israelites attempted to hoard the manna, maggots grew in their stash overnight. We just don't trust that small, sustaining tastes of beauty will carry us, do we? Accepting them as a gift seems too . . . well, easy. We hoard manna and find peanut butter cups (not one, but six). We flee manna's simplicity and grab a J & B bottle and gulp rather than sip it with a sunset. We hoard manna and seek out the woman who seems to really need us—she's so fragile, and we have so much strength to give her. She tells us everything, nothing held back. We reject manna and become necessary to her. We hoard manna and pick up the phone and have countless hours of conversation about someone else, all the while telling ourselves it's important to think through her life because we care so much. We reject manna and find a few solitary hours and spend them with illicit Web sites and masturbation. We flee manna and volunteer for four committees, as opposed to last year's two. We watch *Days of Our Lives*. We mindlessly put on another Christian tea. We become "women who love too much." Most women I know are too busy to even fantasize about having an affair. Does this mean they are more mature than those who do? No, it just means the manna they are hoarding is more appropriate in our culture, especially our church culture, which seems to relish activity.

The path into anything other than the deepened desire stirred by simple provision is control. It's the hallmark of the Fall for us: "Though your desire will be for [literally, your desire will be to control] your husband, he will be your master" (Genesis 3:16). A woman's life is a daily adventure in surrender. I woke up one morning with a piercing awareness that I didn't have any children begging me to make waffles, nor a lover in my bed. I was tempted, for a moment, to crawl back under the covers and make up a dream about a man I care a lot about who has been kind to me. Can you hear how doing so would have been a surrender to boredom and deceit?

Instead of boredom, manna came. I walked out into the dawn to find whispers of red clouds strewn along the horizon. Just above a row of cottonwood trees, a red fox was curled up in the snow, waiting for that first stream of sunlight—she also was waiting. I had a long, uncomfortable talk with God. I reminded Him of how lonely I am, and He held me for a while. Did this manna eradicate my desire? No, it deepened it. But it deepened it toward the heart of God instead of away from Him. The simple provision turned my forgetful heart toward God and away from an attempt to control my desire.

Daily, hourly, we either surrender to boredom in order to gain control of desire or we surrender to the frightening vulnerability of trust. This trust believes that we will not be forgotten and that the desire in our heart will not be dismissed or mishandled. What I said in chapter 1 really is true. We, as women, are cowards. We know there is no more dangerous place than true heart-and-soul intimacy, so we demand guarantees. We seek out excesses that have an illusion of drama but are actually boring compatriots to our agenda—don't stir my heart with simple desire. Illicit sex and alcohol are dangerous, but at least we're the ones calling the shots in how they stir us, or so we think. Dependent relationships hold drama and thrills, but at least we're in charge of where the thrills take us. Dan Allender calls these kinds of substitutes the "flight into indulgence and anesthesia." Curtis and Eldredge call them "less wild lovers." God calls them adultery. I call them the easiest things to choose. Surrender to the unpredictable winds of true intimacy, and we're far too exposed and vulnerable. Our cowardice betrays the true question inside: *Doesn't God care that I'm so exposed and vulnerable out here?*

When we realize where we are (in the alleyway) long enough to let our heart catch up with us—our heart and all it desires— this is the moment of truth. Will we, with stirred desire, flee into a seemingly dangerous world of addiction where desire is perceived to be under our control? Or will we stay put, having our desire stirred with manna, letting it be birthed, grow, expand until all that is left to do is live out the heart cry of Psalm 62?

> *My soul, wait in silence for God only,*
> *For my hope is from Him.*
> *He only is my rock and my salvation,*
> *My stronghold; I shall not be shaken.*
> *On God my salvation and my glory rest;*
> *The rock of my strength, my refuge is in God.*
> *Trust in Him at all times, O people;*
> *Pour out your hearts before Him;*
> *God is a refuge for us.* (Psalm 62:5–8, NASB)

FALSE SHELTERS

Karen carries a hundred pounds of extra weight on her medium frame. Nevertheless, she's always impeccably dressed, with luxurious hair and beautiful skin. She has a warm smile and is able to engage in meaningful conversation with a bright mind. She told me right away that she had come to recognize that her weight was a shield for her, a shelter against her heart. We both knew there was more to it than that. But getting at that "more" proved no easy task. When the conversation turns to Karen, when she is inquired of, her gaze drops. She becomes nervous and flighty. The first four conversations I had with Karen were spent with me trying to inquire of her, and with her making it clear that she had to somehow protect me from whatever was in her heart. At first she tried to convince me there was nothing inside worth pursuing. Then the truth came out: she was afraid that if I saw what was in her heart, it would end up hurting *me*.

Eventually I told her that her attempts to protect me were making me weary and sad. I wondered if I'd ever know her. I asked her when she became so convinced she was an abuser. Stunned and incredulous, she began to tell me her story. She briefly skimmed over the fact that her grandfather and uncle sexually abused her repeatedly. She then went into passionate detail about the neighborhood children she had sought out for sexual pleasure in her adolescence. She was determined to prove to me how reckless she was, as if, had I enough evidence, I would realize how depraved she was, and I would leave her alone.

I couldn't contain my tears. This woman was working so hard to deepen her own sense of shame, she didn't even pause long enough to hear her own story. I asked her where all the other major players in her life were in her story. Who was watching when her uncle was seeking her out? Where was her protection when her grandfather was seducing her with Tootsie Rolls and dolls? Who was a strong enough presence in her life, pursuing how she really was, that the web of deceit and hiding could have been broken down? Who gave her a place of safety?

She came up empty, shocked that it was even a question. I asked her who had enjoyed her just for who she was—who had dreamed with her, played with her, sought her out just because they delighted in her little heart, spirit, and mind. As I painted this picture, she began to soften and remember her heart. There had been a teacher. Someone whose gaze toward her was only of curiosity and delight, with no sexual price to pay. As she described this teacher, she became radiant for a moment. Then the radiance faded as she jumped quickly to remind me of the neighborhood children she had harmed.

I told Karen words could never capture my sorrow for the damage those neighborhood kids experienced from her. But I couldn't talk to her about them until she was willing to truly weep for them. Startled, she questioned me deeply—couldn't I see that those kids were all she cared about? Yes, I said, I could see that they were the focus of her energy. But I told her I wanted to really *weep with her* for those kids, and there was no way I could do that when she was using them as a shield for her own heart. Karen's desire, her fine meal, was finding out that her heart mattered. Simple desire told her that she really did want to be the focus because she wanted to matter to someone. And simple desire told her that she wanted to be forgiven.

Slowly Karen began to see that she had joined hands with evil, just not in the way she thought she had. Was her abuse of those children wrong? Absolutely. Worthy of great punishment. Jesus Himself said it would be better for a person to be tossed into the sea with a millstone hanging around her neck than to cause little ones to mistrust God's care (Mark 9:42). But Karen had joined hands with evil by believing the whisper "You are a ruthless, reckless, dangerous woman. You are not to be trusted. Lock your heart away before you destroy anyone else." This whisper had become her false shelter; her shame over harming those children had become her shield. Karen was far more concerned about not being an abusive woman than she was about seeking God's forgiveness for her crime. It wasn't until she allowed herself to be reminded of her own heart—her desire for legitimate care as a child, her desire to be a loving and strong presence in the lives of the neighborhood kids—it wasn't until she was able to say to me, "I am an abuser," that she was able to drink in the full forgiveness of God and weep clean tears over those neighborhood children. The desire that had been locked away in her heart rose up and destroyed the false shelters of evil. She started to see that in the kingdom she could be a destructive force—destructive against the Enemy himself.

SHELTERS OF FORGETFULNESS

Like Karen, we think we can provide a shelter for ourselves, a shelter from hope itself, a boring shelter of deceit. We make simple desire the enemy. It's too vulnerable for us. This has been going on for as long as there have been enemies. Jerusalem did it. Assyria was an enemy with a ruthless, savage reputation. The proud rulers of Jerusalem boasted about striking a bargain with death to avoid death (literally, making a covenant with Sheol, the land of forgetfulness). As they proclaimed, "The Assyrians can never touch us, for we have built a strong refuge made of lies and deception" (Isaiah 28:15).

We are no different. We hover and chide ourselves for being so foolish as to enjoy life, or we clamor and demand things our way. We fully believe either choice will protect us. But both are lies. Both are deceptions. And both cause our femininity to wither and die. We cannot defend our own hearts.

It's simple, really. We would rather go about the business of taking control of things than feel the threat of the alleyway. We congratulate each other and say, "Oh, Meg, you are so strong. You can handle anything, can't you?") And in just the same way, rather than facing the utter brutality of the Assyrian culture and its threat to her safety, Israel chose to forget. She determined to build a shelter of forgetfulness, of which God said, "I will take the measuring line of justice and the plumb line of righteousness to check the foundation wall you have built. . . . Since it is made of deception, the enemy will come like a flood to sweep it away. I will cancel the bargain you made to avoid death, and I will overturn your deal to dodge the grave" (Isaiah 28:17-18).

God promises to destroy these false shelters. Until that happens, the Enemy attempts to carry our hearts away. This had almost happened to Karen's heart. The enemy of her soul had whispered powerful deceit to her as she hid behind a shelter that wasn't meant to stand up. In our efforts to shelter ourselves from hope, we actually lay ourselves vulnerable before our true Enemy. Evil delights in our clamoring, knowing that it is there that God's goodness can be mocked with our full permission and partnership. Our hovering gives evil an opportunity to malign God's character as we passively listen and agree with the estimation of our situation: we are forgotten.

But it doesn't work. Karen's desire caught up with her, frankly, through simple curiosity. It didn't take much manna—

just me inquiring of her—to strip her of her hovering blankets. Her many attempts at controlling her desire, the least of which was her excessive food intake, failed her. God knew they would. "For you have no place of refuge—the bed you have made is too short to lie on. The blankets are too narrow to cover you" (Isaiah 28:20).

God's loving call in the midst of our false-shelter building is simple: "Remember what I intended for you. Let Me fight the enemies (including your own treatment of your heart) that have robbed you of your joy. Rest in Me as you recall the promise that I will find you." The message is simple, and yet it is said of us, as of Israel, "They will stumble over this simple, straight-forward message" (Isaiah 28:13).

As we take comfort in our clever ways to forget, God reminds us, "Stop fooling yourselves. If you think you are wise by this world's standards, you will have to become a fool so you can become wise by God's standards. For the wisdom of this world is foolishness to God. As the Scriptures say, 'God catches those who think they are wise in their own cleverness'" (1 Corinthians 3:18-19).

WHISPERS IN THE WILDERNESS

As a girl, I could always tell when Mom was heading down the road to despair. As I mentioned, I would stay a few steps ahead of my own heart in order to keep her alive. Over time I realized I was good at it. I would keep her on the phone while she was in the hospital, convincing her that suicide was not the way to go. You can hear the whisper of the Enemy in my life: "You have to be enough, Jan. Come up with more." I joined hands with evil as I determined to be enough for my mom and for my friends. You can imagine me as the junior-high campus counselor. My false shelter was being built brick by brick. As it grew, my true heart faded into the background.

But false shelters, in God's mercy, crumble. Some are crushed. My false shelter was crushed when, in my high-school years, I came home from a late-night concert to find my mom had attempted suicide. Dad was out of town on business, so my sister and I waited out the hours before Mom was out of the woods. Now, think about what this meant for me. It wasn't just a scary, traumatic night. It was the night I had to face the truth that my false shelter had failed me. The crushing of the shelter came quickly—I couldn't come up with more. I couldn't keep Mom alive. She survived the ordeal, but the verdict was in: I wasn't enough.

What a kind mercy! God used the very thing I was most afraid of to prick the balloon of my self-deception. I wasn't enough, and wasn't that a *relief!* Of course, none of this was evident to me until much later in life. God revealed more of His love to me, more of the way He turns our suffering on its head for our good (Romans 8:28). As I developed a new way of seeing my story—as I saw it more through God's lens than from my own limited sight—I began to realize that the most traumatic evening of my life had been used to keep me from being deceived about my own power. Mom's suicide attempt kept me from believing that I had to come through for her or for anyone else.

And I'm a counselor—how crazy is that? I continue to hear the old familiar whisper. It returns at times when I am talking with people in the counseling office. I always know when my soul is not at rest because that's when I start believing I have to come through for people. My clients can tell you when it is happening: I lose my enjoyment of the process, and the whole thing becomes a grueling project. What an amazing calling for a woman who can tend to believe she must be enough! God has placed me in a profession where I am reminded daily that I am not enough. I have to remember that truth, or the counseling process goes nowhere. When I am embracing the truth that I am not enough, my daily work is a beautiful process. When I surrender to that truth, I know evil's whispers are mocked.

Dan Allender writes of these whispers:

> *The evil one delights in severing relationship and demeaning dig-*
> *nity by setting up traps that strip a person of power, promise*
> *(trust) and pleasure in order to incite powerlessness, betrayal and*
> *shame. A loss of power steals a sense of future and hope from a*
> *person. Betrayal cuts the cords of trust and makes faith seem*
> *foolish. And shame mocks desire and degrades pleasure, thus*
> *destroying the impetus and reward of love. Evil's plan is to*
> *destroy the glory of God in man by attempting to steal from him*
> *what is most sacred and most human: faith, hope and love.* [2]

Evil had been attempting to destroy my hope by mocking me
in the powerlessness I felt. If I couldn't keep Mom alive, then I
had no power—at least that's what evil wanted me to believe.
Only a loving God could take the very thing evil intended and
turn it into something for my good. Was I powerless? Yes, but
not in the way I had thought. God used the whole ordeal to
remind me that only the power of His love can keep my heart
alive, no matter what other people choose to do.

Can you hear what happened? I began to realize that my
mother's suicide attempt actually became manna to my soul as a
woman. It was intrusive manna, but it was manna. Manna that
opened my heart and drowned out the whispers of evil. As God
has stripped away my false shelter, He has given me a new way of
looking at things. And He has freed my heart from the lie that I
must come through for people. He took something destined to
make me hard and bitter and turned it into something that brings
gratitude and tenderness as I remember His care for me. My mom
attempts suicide, and God makes it manna—isn't *that* wild?

SIMPLICITY AND LEISURE

There's a passage in *My Utmost for His Highest* that Brent was
urgent about sharing with the men who went on the retreat

where he died. He wanted so much for the men to hear the call of God within them, telling them that they didn't have to try so hard. He wanted to call them away from their busyness to hear God's calling. He did have the chance to share this with them, and it also was read at his funeral. It captured something that was true for him—simplicity and leisureliness. Brent was not free from being driven (none of us are), but he was more on his way than most. The freedom with which he lived life was so refreshing. A passage from Oswald Chambers says this:

> *If we are in communion with God and recognize that He is taking us into His purposes, we shall no longer try to find out what his purposes are. As we go on in the Christian life it gets simpler, because we are less inclined to say—Now why did God allow this and that? Behind the whole thing lies the compelling of God. "There's a divinity that shapes our ends." A Christian is one who trusts the wits and the wisdom of God, and not his own wits. If we have a purpose of our own, it destroys the simplicity and the leisureliness which ought to characterize the children of God.*[3]

Simplicity and leisureliness are implicit in accepting manna as it is given. Leisurely get up each morning, wait for the fog to burn away, and there it is—a blanket of feathery honey cakes. Simple. Gather the two quarts for you and your family and know it will be enough for that day. Simple. No great strain, no confusion, no striving. Simple manna. But always the same. Always honey cakes. Forty years of honey cakes. Forty years of a picture meant to prompt memory of provision and a vision of the land to come. Forty years of a vulnerable place meant to stir desire for the living God.

A SIMPLE REMINDER

When I met Sherry, she had been in just about every treatment program for anorexia in the West, including a ranch that specializes in the long-term treatment of eating disorders. Like most women with her struggle, she could easily have taught university classes on nutrition, exercise, and the dynamics of the eating disorder itself. She didn't need to understand what the problem was. She could articulate the characteristics of her disorder, reducing and mapping out her heart, with great detail.

She was doing better with her food (meaning she was allowing herself one nutritious meal each day and maintaining her lithe weight). She had more energy, her depression was lifting, and she had enough courage to enter into a dating relationship with a man who made her laugh. So, why did she need to see me, another in a long string of counselors? She knew she was stuck—bored—and didn't like it. I told her that if she realized she didn't want to be bored, then we were already well on our way to knowing her heart, not just mapping it out.

As Sherry told me her story, it became clear that she was the most powerful person in her family. The tiniest whisper of a young woman, and yet she called all the shots. Family members tiptoed around her. She knew that even though she was doing better, her addictive and destructive behavior continued to threaten those around her.

Her boyfriend, the one who made her laugh, didn't do that. He was undaunted by her culinary games, and he seemed genuinely interested in her. For the first time Sherry was being asked to offer her heart, not just a rendition of her heart. And Sherry was so afraid that this man would flee when he finally saw what was inside of her. She felt she was simply too much. She fought being clingy and manipulative.

Sherry's desire was simple. She wanted to know that there was something lovely about her heart, without any gymnastics, that would keep this young man. And she wanted to know that she wasn't too much for him. As she continued to let him in, she softened. It was a slow transformation from an outline of a woman to the fullness of a woman. It was a transformation from control to trust. Robin Norwood says, "If you have ever found yourself obsessed with a man, you may have suspected that the root of that obsession was not love, but fear . . . fear of being unlovable and unworthy, fear of being ignored or abandoned or destroyed."[4] We do just about anything to alleviate this fear. We create all kinds of diversions, smoke screens, and chaos just to keep from having to face our greatest fear: Are we lovely? The answer to this question can be found only in the quiet gathering of manna.

Norwood describes a woman who had a history of choosing destructive relationships:

> *She had to learn to simply be in the company of men whom she considered nice, even if she also found them a little boring. Boredom is the sensation that women who love too much so often experience when they find themselves with a "nice man": no bells peal, no rockets explode, no stars fall from heaven. In the absence of excitement they feel antsy, irritable, and awkward, a generally uncomfortable state that is covered over with the label boredom. . . . Because she was used to excitement and pain, struggle and victory or defeat, an interchange that lacked these powerful components felt too tame to be important, and unsettling as well.* [5]

That's what happens—isn't it?—when we surrender to manna. We have to stop and be alone with our hearts long enough to face our fears. Manna is a simple reminder of God's love, a daily wooing of our hearts. Manna is obvious if we let it be. Like a lover who places love notes in the open, only to see his beloved too preoccupied to notice, God places manna in obvious places. The message to Israel was simple: "So the LORD will spell out his message for them again, repeating it over and over, a line at a time, in very simple words. Yet they will stumble over this simple, straightforward message" (Isaiah 28:13).

MANNA'S PLACE IN THE TABERNACLE

No wonder manna was one of the items placed in the ark of the covenant, along with the Law of God given to Moses. The ark was the place where God chose to take up residence with His people—a picture of His ever-present care and faithful sojourning with them. In the tabernacle, the ark was placed in the Holy of Holies, the one place where only the high priest could enter to offer sacrifices for sin, and that only once a year. It was here that manna was placed as a reminder.

Our lives become so cluttered so quickly. We forget. We expend energy hoarding relationships, refining our reputation, becoming masters at organization, but we forget we're being sustained. We forget God is sojourning with us. We need to be reminded. The Law is a reminder of what God requires of us in order for Him to maintain relationship with us; the manna is a reminder of how He makes provision for us, the very ones who break His Law. Both address our predicament outside the garden.

But only the stone tablets were in the ark when it was transferred to Solomon's temple (1 Kings 8:9). Shortly after that, another item was added to the ark: Aaron's rod. Of all the rods representing the twelve tribes of Israel, this rod was the only symbol of authority that did not wither and die (Hebrews 9:4). Aaron's rod blossomed, bearing fresh almonds, "proving once and for all," says Judson Cornwall, "the question of the priesthood is to be determined solely by Jehovah. Jesus was totally rejected by men, both as prophet and priest. Although he was cut off at the cross God resurrected Him and gave him fruitfulness."[6]

The ark carried manna—the picture of the simple provision that sustains us in our wandering. And manna was replaced by a budding rod that points to Jesus. Manna is the taste; Jesus is the meal. Jesus is the fulfillment of all the unmet desire stirred from every taste of manna.

Jesus said this about Himself to the crowds in Capernaum:

"You shouldn't be so concerned about perishable things like food. Spend your energy seeking the eternal life that I, the Son of Man, can give you. For God the Father has sent me for that very purpose."

They replied, "What does God want us to do?"

Jesus told them, "This is what God wants you to do: Believe in the one he has sent."

They replied, "You must show us a miraculous sign if you want us to believe in you. What will you do for us? After all, our ancestors ate manna while they journeyed through the wilderness! As the Scriptures say, 'Moses gave them bread from heaven to eat.'"

Jesus said, "I assure you, Moses didn't give them bread from heaven. My Father did. And now he offers you the true bread from heaven. The true bread of God is the one who comes down from heaven and gives life to the world."

"Sir," they said, "give us that bread every day of our lives."

Jesus replied, "I am the bread of life. No one who comes to me will ever be hungry again." (John 6:27–35)

There *is* satisfaction for a woman's heart. Simplicity and leisureliness deepen our passion for more. The manna we gather deepens our passion for Christ's merciful presence.

Manna shows up each day in little foxes and sunrises. Emerson said, "The sky is the daily bread of the eyes." Oh, so true—especially in the West, the sky is always there, and it is always changing. It is always manna. Lingering over a cup of coffee with a friend, taking time—making time—to actually inquire of her, is manna. Preparing a tray of sweet william seedlings so they will flourish come spring is manna. Strolling through an art gallery with your kids. Relishing a quiet time of worship. Taking the hand of an elderly person and seeing light return to her eyes. Drinking in other perspectives in a reading group. Noticing the back lighting of the setting sun, making field grasses translucent. Running along a river and spotting a deer. Manna is everywhere. Every day.

And along the way, the Bread of Life gives Himself, not merely to cause us to hunger, but to fulfill our desire. Jesus takes unmet desire and intrudes into it to surprise us with His love. He takes our losses and weeps with us, comforting and feeding us until we are strengthened for the journey. He takes the abuse and betrayal we suffer, and He rages on our behalf against the evil committed against us. He takes our weary souls and stirs our desire, and then, after we've stumbled away from Him, He reveals that this desire can be met only through His love, in the power of His Spirit. Along the way, the Bread of Life compels us to worship.

We can't respond to the call of God without responding to desire, and desire whispers each day, calling us away from our indulgences. When we respond and follow, eating His bread and drinking His cup, we are living out of passion, sharing in His sufferings, giving Him our very lives—worshiping Him in unexpected ways. And we aren't bored.

～6

DAILY DESIRE

You would call and I would answer,
and you would yearn for me, your handiwork.
— JOB

Hope is a thing with feathers /
that perches in the soul / and sings the
tune —/ without the words / and never stops at all.
— EMILY DICKINSON

By painting I pour out not only
what I see, but what I wish to see.
— JESSICA ROYAL, AGE THIRTEEN

What is the big deal, exactly, with desire? Women especially
need to consider this question because it was desire gone astray
that caused us to lose Eden. Desire gone astray leads to gam-
bling and affairs. Yet desire is the very place where God daily
reveals His Son to us, where spiritual freedom is born. Meister
Eckhart says, "Wherever God the Father declares his word within

the soul, wherever the place of this birth may be, and wherever the soul may be receptive to this event, *this must be the purest and most noble and most tender place* the soul can offer"[1] (emphasis added). This is the essence of feminine desire.

Can you hear how *reflective* desire is of our femininity? It is the center of who we are as women. Put aside all thoughts of your functionality for a moment, all the roles you play as wife, mother, carpooler, organizer, employee, manager. What we're talking about here is your pulse. It's the little girl's heart that can't wait to show off her new dance steps—pure exuberance. It's the spunk to climb a tree, the peacefulness to daydream there. It's your spark ignited by romance, arousing tender longings. It is the passion that blazes in intimacy, inviting a surrender of self. It is everything noble that compels a woman to offer herself to others so they can enter. Our tenderness is entered in order to conceive new life. Desire makes us fertile. Desire conceives and gives birth to life. Without it we are barren.

GIVING BIRTH

It was the last conversation Brent and I would ever have. It was spontaneous; we both had full schedules, but we decided to take advantage of our lunch breaks and head to a little café downtown that he had been drawn to because of its umbrellas. It was a windy spring day in Colorado, the kind that makes you second-guess your choice to eat outside. But we ate our sandwiches and bundled up in our jackets and talked for a while.

We chatted about the comings and goings of people in our community of friends. Brent talked in typical fashion of his love for his family and of the plans they were making. Suddenly, he became very earnest. When Brent got earnest, he would slightly cock his head, and it would shake with a small tremor as he waited for a response. He asked me, "How *are* you?" He really wanted to know. My threshold wasn't especially high that day, and I teared up. I tried to explain the difficulty of continuing day to day as a single woman, especially as I give of myself in the counseling office, fighting for other people's marriages.

Brent listened and leaned forward, and with simple focus, he said to me, "Jan, I'm so sorry that you are having to give life this way." He knew my longings for marriage and children. "But one thing is sure," he said. "You will have a very special place in heaven."

We all have within us the desire to give life. The bodies of women were crafted to conceive and bear children, so obviously we have a special affinity for the giving of life. There is a force that transcends these natural longings, deepens them even, to the point that we yearn to provide nourishment for others. We were meant to give life.

Brent's words gave me strength because they revealed an understanding of what is asked of us as women. He acknowledged that of course I longed to give myself fully to a man and to know the joy and agony of childbirth. He also acknowledged that there was something more primary going on for me: I wanted to give life any way I could. He knew I didn't want to give up; he knew I was just weary, aching.

Sue Monk Kidd says, "Whenever new life grows and emerges, darkness is crucial to the process. Whether it's the caterpillar in the chrysalis, the seed in the ground, the child in the womb, or the True Self in the soul, there's always a time of waiting in the dark."[2] That's where I was. I was groaning along the way in the labor of my life story. And I had the luxury of someone noticing. We all want that, don't we?

And that's how desire is, right? It causes a groaning whether we are literally in labor or not. Desire reminds us that we were made to dance with Baryshnikov but that today we are learning our steps with sore legs. We were meant to captivate like Jacqueline Kennedy Onassis, but today we are searching for a shred of grace. We were meant to bear life, but today we are aching—the birth is coming. Kidd goes on to say, "When Jesus selected this beautiful feminine metaphor, he wanted us to grasp the importance not only of new birth but of how that birth happens. I think he was implying that with every birth there is a womb, and if we want to find the inner kingdom, we will have to enter the place of waiting, darkness, and incubation."[3] She's right. Desire has to be given a place to grow. That's what Brent was recognizing for me—this place is usually one of waiting with little light.

Desire germinates in the most tender and noble place in our soul, and what grows there is beyond our keeping. One woman proclaimed the obvious after the birth of her daughter: "It was all much bigger than me!" As our desire grows, as the anticipation of the birth deepens, we have to surrender to something much bigger than ourselves.

Birth just sort of takes over, doesn't it? We have to show up, but it is going to happen whether we agree to it or not. So, as God stirs our feminine desire, we are invited—or shall I say compelled?—to engage our hearts in the story He is telling. We give birth by giving ourselves over to His intentions for us, by allowing Him to enter our hearts, stirring and deepening our desire for more—our desire for Him. So, how do we do that? It may sound funny, but we can't start unless we admit we are with child. We start by living our own story.

ANOTHER'S STORY

Have you ever been caught perpetuating an urban myth? You know, those stories woven into conversations at dinner parties or at the office. They all have a certain drama and a can-you-believe-that? tone to them. Problem is, when the person telling the story is nailed down on her source . . . well, there usually isn't one. It's a friend of a friend of a friend. The stories get passed around, and the shred of truth that perhaps was there in the beginning is now embellished beyond recognition.

Several years ago I was such a perpetuator. I had been telling a story for over fifteen years that I considered *my* story. I loved telling it because it always brought lots of laughs from my audience. I spoke of how my mom's friend Kathleen had visited the little mountain community where Robert Redford was directing the film *The Milagro Beanfield War*. Kathleen went into a little ice-cream store and purchased a cone when suddenly she realized Robert Redford was behind her in line. Flustered, she went out to her car and tried to calm down enough to go back in and get his autograph. Suddenly she realized she had forgotten her change at the counter. *Perfect!* she thought, and she charged back into the store, only to be met with knowing grins from everyone, including Redford. Bewildered, she asked the clerk for her change. He gladly gave it to her, but as she went to put it in her purse, she realized why all the grins—she had put her ice-cream cone in her purse.

Cute story, right? Well, I told that story to Brent and Ginny at dinner one night. We all laughed. Then the next week I found an envelope on my desk. Inside the envelope was an article from *Good Housekeeping* about urban myths. The example the author cited was my story, only on the East Coast and with Paul Newman. I was incredulous! I still believed it was *my* story! (I'm a little thick sometimes.) I even called my mom and asked her about Kathleen's experience. "I don't recall anything about that, honey." Shoot. I called Kathleen after fifteen years. "That never happened to me, Jan." Sigh. My ego was further demolished when, a week later, someone told me she heard Kathie Lee Gifford ramble on with this cute story she had heard about Paul Newman . . . *Auggh!*

Where had I come to the conclusion that the story I was telling was true? When did I adopt it as my own without permission? This happens easily in the desolate and boring place. We start telling someone else's story because we don't want our own. The dark incubation of our desire seems like too much to ask, so we turn our attention elsewhere to tame our desire. When we do not have a deep remembrance of the eyes of God toward us, we scramble, trying to come up with ways to make the desert bearable day to day. Rather than looking ahead to how He may surprise us, how He might show up, we look around and find bits and pieces of other people's dramas to keep us entertained. We start finding life in other people's stories.

Isn't that what our fascination with drama and violence is all about? And isn't that what is tapped into when we flip the channel during the afternoon hours to get just one glimpse of Jessica on *One Life to Live?* Other people's stories are so much more intriguing than our own, and if we can enter them with no personal cost, so much the better. The problem is, when we start living on other people's stories, we start to lose our own. And our own story, in that tender place of longing, day to day, is what carries God's message for us.

Eve certainly screwed up the story. The story God gave to Adam had been passed on to her, and as she was convinced it wasn't enough, she altered the story for her own purposes. She and the serpent did an inelegant dance of deception, the serpent taking one step ("Did God really say you may not eat of any fruit in the garden?"), then Eve taking one ("Of course we may eat it. . . . It's only the fruit from the tree at the center of the garden that we are not allowed to eat. God says we must not eat it or even touch it, or we will die."). The serpent started stepping on her toes as he came in for the kill: "You won't die! . . . God knows that your eyes will be opened when you eat it. You will become just like God, knowing everything, both good and evil" (Genesis 2:1-5). The story Eve had been given by God wasn't good enough for her, so she went after another one. She was convinced, and she lost her story.

INELEGANT DANCES

Can you hear how we do this inelegant dance every day? The best example is gossip. This is the classic path of least resistance for women. We're at lunch with a friend, and we feel a bit insecure about what we have to give to the conversation, so we turn to something juicy about Marie, a mutual acquaintance. As we talk about Marie and the struggle she and her husband have been having financially, our hearts deflate and we realize we have lost our spark, but we continue this inelegant dance. We drive away from the lunch with a gnawing discomfort, like we have just reached for deceptive fruit. We have been deceived. We chatted and bantered with our friend, but she knows nothing more of us than she did before. And we know nothing more of her. Our story has been lost, and we drive away barren. Gossip steals life from relationships.

The same is true of fantasy. Our stories aren't quite enough, so we flee into a crafted world of romance, seduction, sexual pleasure, or just being noticed. I'm talking about the fantasies we create as we stand in line at the mall, as we ride the elevator at work, as we wait for our children to finish on the jungle gym, as we sit in a car when the music is blaring and no one is interested in talking. In these moments we disconnect from the story we are living and make up a story we think will ease our ache.

I speak to sweet Christian ladies who have fantasies that would make Fabio blush. Some are erotic. Some are charged memories, intentionally replayed like a movie. Some are filled with slow and repetitive tenderness. What's going on here? These fantasies take an enormous amount of creativity and energy, even at a stoplight. When we probe a little, it doesn't take long to find that the woman with such rich fantasies is a passionate woman; she just doesn't realize it. She is ashamed and confused by the force and vibrancy of her desire. That's the point. She has to be ashamed because she has turned something lovely from her story (her desire) into something illicit.

It isn't just sweet women who are ashamed. Many women carry a secret belief that if their deepest desires were unveiled, people would shrink back, no one could handle them. The secret belief is *If these desires are not bridled, broken, and corralled, then watch out—I will become a romance novel heroine, a prostitute, or a sexual predator.* You see the problem? She doesn't stay with her own story and desire long enough to realize she is passionate for good things. What's missing is sitting at the stoplight and allowing her heart to yearn for some deeper connection with her husband. What's missing is standing in line at the grocery store and being awakened by God as she remembers her tender desire for a good friend. As she stays in her own story, those longings deepen her ache and suddenly she is, again, in need of God. She is passionate for good things—the good, unpredictable, uncontrollable things of God and relationship. As she flees into fantasy, it never dawns on her that, were she to stay in her own story for a while, God might find her in her ache—she might become a captivating woman who lives the gospel with a fire desperately needed in the church today. Fantasy steals passion from our hearts, so it steals life from the church.

You can see where this takes us. As we forget our own stories, we become frauds. We lose sight of the greater story God is telling through us, and we flee to the path of least resistance. It takes courage to live the story we are given. The Israelites, just months from witnessing the parting of the Red Sea (a story even Charlton Heston couldn't quite capture), wanted the security of bondage again—it was preferable to manna in the wilderness on the way to promise.

Gerald May says, "We naturally seek the least threatening ways of trying to satisfy our longing for God, ways that protect our sense of personal power and require the least sacrifice."[4] This was true for the Israelites; it's true for us in fantasy and gossip; and it has been true for women for centuries. Gomer wasn't longing to be back with Hosea. "I guess it would be better for me with him than it is for me now," she says (see Hosea 2:7). The prodigal wasn't really longing to go home; he was just sick of pig slop. We will do just about anything to avoid the story we're in. God graciously lets us flee into our fraudulent miniseries, trying to convince ourselves that we don't need His company. But He waits for us to stumble home eventually.

We cannot possibly know what it is we desire until God

shows us our hearts in surprising ways. He hears Israel's complaints; He provides passage into Canaan anyway. He sees Gomer's wandering heart; He draws her into the wilderness with kindness and renames her children. His heart is broken by the rejection of His Son; He runs down the road anyway, with an expression of delight worthy of the best of parties. He hears our gossip, sees our fantasies; He sees how we flee our story; and He puts on the feast for us. This is our story. And for us as women—even for us as lonely, yearning women—that is cause for celebration.

OUR STORY

Don Hudson tells of a tradition that can be found in some Jewish homes.[5] The Jewish father has as his aim the prompting of questions in the hearts of his children, drawing them out to discover the truth for themselves. In this spirit, a father may assign his children certain roles in a small drama played out around the dinner table. One child is given the role of the simple child; one is the foolish child; one is assigned to be the wise child; and one, the evil child. The children are prompted on what their role and response is to be. The father then recites the family's heritage—where they came from, what visions Grandfather lived for, what has mattered to the family through the generations, where the father hopes to see the family go, what his dreams and wishes for the children are. The father then turns to each child and asks for a response to all that has been said.

The first couple of responses are predictable. The simple child yawns and asks if she might go and watch television for a while. The foolish child rolls her eyes and says, "Dad, you're done telling the story. What difference does it make?"

The next two are not so easy to discern. The father turns to the wise child, who responds: "Thanks for telling me *our* story, Daddy." Then, as he turns to the evil child, he hears, "Thank you for telling me *my* story, Father."

The evil child wanted her heritage to begin and end with her. The wise child knew her story couldn't be separated from her heritage. Our stories are given to us by God; they are never meant to impact only us. Rodney Clapp says that the New Testament doesn't even imagine an autonomous person.[6] As we live our lives in the Valley of Achor (the "Valley of Trouble," Hosea 2:15), consumed with our own stories and the losses they hold, we lose sight of the majestic way God weaves our paths with others in the desert. We make the Valley of Achor an endless door of revisited sorrow rather than allowing God to transform it into a door of hope as we bump up against other people. Sue Monk Kidd says of this, "As the True Self is born within us, the initial movement of soul is from the collective 'they' to the ground of an authentic 'I.' That's holy ground, yet God calls us to a ground even holier: God calls us from the authentic 'I' toward a compassionate 'we.'"[7] Relationship with God and the people He brings into our lives becomes the door of hope.

COLLIDING STORIES

Sit back now because I'm going to tell you a story. Simply put, this is a story you may not believe, but I need to tell it anyway.

When Susan first came into my office as a new client, I knew I was in trouble. Craig Barnes says, "Jesus is constantly moving us away from places where we would prefer to stay."[8] As Susan told me about herself, I knew the truth of those words. I wasn't afraid of her, really. I was just strangely aware that something was in store for both of us.

As the process unfolded, it became clear that this would be a long-distance journey. No simple processing of misplaced angst for this one. Right off, it became clear that Susan had lived a personal hell as a child in the hands of her own family, who were members of a cult committed to the appeasement and worship of Satan. They were all too quick to place their daughter's welfare on the altar of their pursuit of power. Susan was now thirty years old, and every day was a battle for her.

Our journey began. It didn't take long for me to see I was in over my head. A colleague brought in some consultants to help train us — people who are called to work in this realm. What happened during that training time shut me up. These counselors approached working with my client with the utmost humility and care. They were the handmaidens of God as they relied on His guidance in how to address her soul. We had the privilege of watching as she courageously invited Jesus to take her on a tour of her own soul. As He did this, He slowly reclaimed the territory of her soul that had been held captive by evil for so long. The deception (she described it as "evil structures" that had been built around her heart) was blown apart by the light of the love of God. It was worship. It was enough to make me a charismatic.

Please continue to sit back. The story goes on.

Susan's greatest fear was that she would never trust God. This fear was at the forefront of her thinking as she dealt with memories of a time during college when members of the cult tracked her down and abducted her in a university parking lot. They took her to an abandoned area, and there, for an entire night, they put her through rigorous torture intended to get her to renounce her faith in Christ. The torture was so heinous and ongoing that she barely survived — they left her for dead in the tumbleweeds. She was found in time to get her to a hospital. But after she was discharged, she dropped out of school and wandered the streets for many months, a broken and confused bundle of fear. She was convinced her heart would now harden over forever. Susan was a joy to work with — she was softhearted and timid — but she was also fully convinced of her hardheartedness. There was no convincing her otherwise.

So the day came. A day like any other. Susan came into my office; we chatted about life and she began to tell me a little of what was going on for her. Suddenly there came a strange look into her eyes, one I had not seen before. She interrupted herself and asked, "When were you in Africa?"

Startled, I told her I had been a missionary in southern Africa in the late 1980s.

"Yeah, yeah," she mumbled as she obviously was remembering something. "Did you drive a white car? A two-door white car that broke down all the time?"

At this point I'm thinking, *How did she know? What is going on here?* For all the journeying we had done together, she knew little or nothing of my personal life or past. I told her that, yes, I had driven a two-door white car. Yes, it broke down frequently. It was the joke of our team, my car.

Susan was energized now. "Was your car often full of black, brown, and white people?

It was South Africa, I'm thinking. *But how did she know?*

Susan proceeded to paint for me scenes from my life in Africa that she had no way of knowing. To the smallest detail. She described an area of Soweto where I used to drop off young people; it was an area I had no business being in. "You were really naïve," she said. We laughed. But as we laughed, I was completely unnerved by what was transpiring.

She paused, and with tears in her eyes, she said, "Jan, it was *you.*"

"*What* was me?" I asked.

"It was you who I prayed for."

"What?"

"During those days . . . after I was left for dead. . . . You know, I could hardly get around, let alone pray. I had no desire to pray. But God kept giving me these visions of a curly-haired woman in Africa who I was supposed to pray for. I remember trying to ignore it, but I couldn't. I prayed for you. A lot. I saw those scenes from your life, so I knew how to pray. I'm remembering now that I felt nuts praying for some woman I didn't know."

Silence.

Susan and I sat in silence for twenty minutes as the reality of what she had said penetrated us. Finally, I began, "So, what you are telling me is, you responded to the heart of God on behalf of someone else, someone you didn't even know, in the midst of the most painful season of your life. And you're telling me that the woman you prayed for was me?" I knew it was me.

There was nothing to say. We dissolved in worship. Remember, after her abduction and torture, she was convinced she would always be hardhearted. As she realized that she had prayed for me—as she remembered that she had prayed for *anyone*—it was as if God had said, "Hardhearted, are you?" At the same time He gave me a gift of His intimate sight and care that I can never repay. He loved me enough to prompt a total stranger to pray for me as I roamed the countries of southern Africa. And He had the finesse (or sense of humor) to bring that woman into my counseling office ten years later.

Thank you for listening to this story. You can sit up now. I've told you this story because we all have stories of awe, stories that prompt our vision for what is possible with the wild heart of God.

No Woman Is an Island

Our stories, the stories of others, and the way our stories collide can add up to increased desire and increased hope if we let them. Do we injure and disappoint each other along the way? Absolutely. But without the intersection of lives—without the "our story" of Christianity—we silently hand ourselves over to enemy occupation. This is the insight Kathleen Norris stumbled into when thinking about joining a church: "The church is like the Incarnation itself, a shaky proposition. It is a human institution, full of ordinary people, sinners like me, who say and do cruel, stupid things. But it is also a divinely inspired institution, full of good purpose, which partakes of a unity far greater than the sum of its parts. That is why it is called the body of Christ."[9]

Sacred stories are reserved for those who bump into each other out in the alleyway. Only the body of Christ could hold up such a story. Only God could have thought it up. No soap opera, gossip tidbit, or fantasy could even come close. The story

I have told you is sacred because it echoes the love God has for me and my client. It echoes the story He's trying to tell through both our lives. And truthfully, we had to collide in order for it to happen, and we both had to be willing to let it be our story. That's a large part of the battle for our hearts as women—simply keeping engaged in the story line and aware of the other players.

GUERRILLAS OF GRACE

In the book *Guns and Rain* anthropologist David Lan takes us into the bush country of Rhodesia. The book describes the guerrilla warfare that would eventually bring independence to the country we now know as Zimbabwe. Its narrative of the history of this beautiful African nation is chilling. It documents the ancestor worship believed to be responsible for the country's freedom.

Imagine bands of African nationalists out in the bush, plotting their warfare strategies against the British colonialists. The British had guns and ammunition. The African soldiers had little more than spiritual guidance they rallied from the spirits of their ancestors through sacrifices and rituals. And the African soldiers won. When they paraded through the streets of Salisbury (now Harare), they displayed enormous banners with African faces on them—the faces of ancestors to whom they paid homage for their victory. Streets in Harare now bear the names of those people esteemed to have given their posthumous guidance in the war. It is almost inconceivable in our Western worldview, but Zimbabwe's history as a nation rests upon dark spiritual forces.

We sometimes don't realize the guerrilla warfare we are in as women. We are out in the bush, fighting for our independence, but we've forgotten what independence we really want. Sadly, throughout history we've joined forces with evil all too often in order to gain some freedom for ourselves. And just like the African soldiers, we quickly learn that it works. We may not rely on ancestors, but we are taken in by the same evil that has seduced women for centuries. It may glare at us as we proclaim our reproductive rights, but it whispers as we efficiently separate our hearts from those around us. There is a seductive quality to being an independent woman, whether it is strategizing in the boardroom of a corporate tower, running the tightest ship of a home, or being known as a capable ministry person. But this kind of freedom isn't what our deepest desire is telling us we need.

The battle is being waged over those things that make us uniquely female, the things of our deepest desire: our tenderness, our strength, our creativity, our winsomeness, our insight and intuition. When these qualities flourish in us, evil is threatened more than at any other time. These qualities are stifled as much or more in church programs that foster automaton Christian women (and prescriptive Christian mothering) as they are in the feminist movement.

When you're around a woman with these qualities, her life proclaims the redemptive power of Jesus Christ—if evil cannot keep a woman hard, shrouded, rigid, pressured, and preoccupied, it has lost. Remember, this battle is about love. Gerald May says, "There is no power and no condition that God's grace cannot penetrate with love. God can indeed, then, work through the power of evil."[10]

My client, Susan, and I would never have had the surprising taste of God's love had He not taken evil's intentions and turned them upside down. Evil does not want a woman's heart to be set ablaze with the love of Christ through the Holy Spirit, so she is offered all kinds of deals in the bush. The good news is, love can turn those deals into something beautiful.

And you may not know this, but you aren't meant to win the battle yourself. Oh, there's no question you'll shed blood and be wounded if you engage your heart in loving, if you're determined to give birth. But we forget what the battle is about, and especially what the battle is over. The battle is over your heart. We forget that we—our hearts—are the battleground. But the battle is not ours to win or lose. Ephesians 6:12 tells us, "Our struggle is not against flesh and blood, but against . . . the powers of this dark world" (NIV). The battle being waged in the heavenlies is over you—over you being either lost or found in your story, day to day. And your heart can be found only by His love.

So often I have heard women proclaim with militant fervor that they must "tear down every speculation and every thought that sets itself up against the knowledge of Christ" (2 Corinthians 10:5). They must "take every thought captive to the obedience of Christ." Is this part of the battle? Absolutely! But these good soldiers are becoming hardened and battle-weary. If the battle is up to you, then you had better be a good soldier. But it isn't up to you. Jesus shed precious blood to make sure of that. So you can show up—you must show up—and you must tear down those obstacles in the way. But it is a tearing down of everything that sets itself up against the knowledge of Jesus' love for you. That's the battle, really, for us as women. Rest in the knowledge that Jesus is fighting on your behalf.

BUSH DEALS

One deal is to become a woman whose sweetness is artificial and leaves a bitter aftertaste. This woman always seems to try hard to be encouraging and nice, but you wonder if you could ever get an honest opinion out of her. It's sad, isn't it? If she understood the battle for her heart, she might be able to enjoy a belly laugh over a glass of wine. She has lost her tenderness to evil's counterfeit of saccharin sweetness.

Another deal is to take on an obvious mantle of power. This woman runs the show, and nobody dares question her competence. If this woman understood the lengths Jesus went to in His quest to have her heart, she might allow herself to be caught off guard. But for now, this woman has lost her strength to evil's control.

Yet another deal is to trade intuition for naïveté. This woman can often be heard saying, "Really?" with a tone of utter shock. She is dumbfounded when her teenager becomes pregnant. She is astounded that her friend would have an affair. She barricades herself with Christian radio, Christian bookstores, Christian doctors, but she doesn't know the battle is for her—over her. She doesn't see the beauty of the story, that blood was shed for her wandering heart. She has closed her eyes to the realities of evil in her own life, so the enemy becomes anything "out there" that threatens her illusions. Wouldn't it be incredible for her to trust her intuition, which tells her this is a battle she cannot fight for herself? Wouldn't it be wonderful to have her tell you she is struggling with something? If she did, her heart and the hearts of her family members wouldn't be so vulnerable to attack.

Another deal made in the bush is to trade genuine sight—eyes willing to see all that evil is up to, all that God is up to, and the importance of the battle—for arrogance. This woman believes she has figured out what Christianity is all about because she has wrapped her mind around the Scriptures and can explain everything. She is the good little soldier, but I can't imagine what she'll be like in five or six years after battling from her own resources an enemy she's not meant to defeat by herself.

Every deal we make with evil is dealt with the heart, fought with our mind, soul, and strength, and paid for with our femininity. What Eckhart calls the "most noble and most tender place the soul can offer" becomes more and more hidden as we give our hearts away to counterfeits. That's what the battle is, right? It is a battle to keep the love alive between God and ourselves, a battle to keep us from becoming barren. Gerald May says, "Let us never forget that deserts are gardens of courtship as well as fields of battle. Struggle with attachment can be seen as warfare with an insidious enemy, or it can be seen as a romance in which the soul seeks the beloved one for whom it thirsts."[11]

There's no question that as we show up in our own stories, as we enter the battle, allowing God to fight for us, we will take bullets. Julian of Norwich wrote that our wounds become the womb.

As we take a shot from someone who does not understand us, can we allow the wound to remind us of the spit that hit Jesus' face, the insults His ears couldn't help hearing? When we are betrayed, can the wound become the place of birth to a greater understanding of what Jesus experiences with us every day?

Jesus is fighting the battle, going out in front in order to fight on our behalf, in order to free our captive hearts. All of this actually frees us to enter life, to engage, to take risks, to offer substance, creativity, intuition, and beauty more than we ever have before. We will take bullets and we will bleed, but He does not intend for us to fight the battle alone. He is fighting for us, and He is fighting over us. And He takes evil's offers and turns them upside down and inside out until something beautiful comes out of the mess.

HOPE'S POWER TO TRANSFORM OUR STORIES

We bear our stories uniquely as women. Our hearts cry, "Let me give life, but let this labor be over!" That's my story, and I'm guessing it is yours as well. But you have different desires; you've heard different messages; you've had different beautiful intrusions; you've made different deals. Your labor is not mine. And that's the beauty of it, isn't it? We need each other desperately. We need to know our passions are not merely illicit, to be disciplined and reined in. We need to know our hearts have something to offer. Henri Nouwen says, "The whole meaning of Christian community lies in offering each other a space in which we wait for what we have already seen."12 We need to be reminded of how God is showing up unannounced in other women's lives so we don't feel so crazy and alone.

Our daily desire can sound like this: *I hope God will tell His story through me. I hope my hard heart will soften. I hope His love shows through me in spite of myself. I hope my life will make a difference in this weary world, bringing refreshment and life to those without it. I hope to be surprised as God's glory shows up unexpectedly; I hope to have eyes to see His kindness and His humor. I hope to draw out the heart of a person with curiosity rather than alienate with my spiritual pride.*

And when our hope sounds like this, then we, as women, have entered His story. It's a story of betrayal, blood, asphyxiation, bullets, bush deals, loss, and death. It's a story of birth, healing, love, resurrection, forgiveness, and restoration. It is a story that began long before the garden and was played out in Eden's piercing beauty. It continues here day to day in sacred and mundane moments, and will be played out throughout eternity. It is our story. He longs for us to show up.

≈7

YEARNING FOR HEAVEN

Even the mountains seem to know you're gone.
—FERNANDO ORTEGA

Lord, enlarge the expanse of my heart.
—ANONYMOUS PSALMIST

Eternal in joy for a day's training on earth.
—BLAISE PASCAL

So you show up in your story. You respond to desire. You ache and groan. The good news is, the ache you feel is meant to expand your heart, not paralyze it. When the composer of Psalm 119 pleaded, "Lord, enlarge the expanse of my heart" (a literal rendering of verse 32), it was almost as if he were pleading for a place to put all the desire that was within him. He knew it felt like there wasn't enough room in his heart to hold the desires of earth, but somehow he knew it could, and had to, grow and make room for the desire of hope and the expanse of heaven.

It is a rare person who can (without despairing) walk the soil between unmet longings here on earth and the anticipation of having those desires realized in heaven. When our lives collide with such a person, our thirst for that place—our eternal party, feast, rest, and work—increases. We glimpse his or her hope and figure it must be worth the wait.

My friend Brent was such a person. "I wonder whether there is on earth anything as exquisitely lovely as a brilliant mind aglow with the love of God," wrote A. W. Tozer.[1] That was Brent's impact. He was my friend and my counseling partner in the battle for hearts. Seventeen years my senior, he led me with respect and humility; never did I feel condescended by him. He would often tell me with a wry smile that I had an "old soul"— a concept he cavalierly borrowed from Native American tradition. I smiled deep inside to hear those words. Somehow I knew he saw me; he understood.

And now he is gone. Out of reach. Blaise Pascal says, "Nothing stays for us." I am beginning to understand that our yearning for heaven, the deepest hope we have in our expanding hearts, begins with wanting what is out of reach. Sounds contrary—doesn't it?—to the lessons we're taught: Be content with what you have. Face reality. Wake up and smell the coffee. Or as I heard Dr. Laura say to someone the other day, "Don't go around desiring what you don't have. If you're miserable, it is your fault for wanting something that isn't." There's some truth to this, of course, because what we don't have—lover, friend, health, reputation—could no more fill us than could one bite of filet mignon or one sip of Château St. Michele. But if we direct our lives solely by what we can see and understand, we lose mystery, we lose the *metanoia* of Christianity, and most of all we lose our deepest hope—the desire for what C. S. Lewis called "the far-off country." He says, "I am almost committing an indecency. I am trying to rip open the inconsolable secret in each one of you—the secret which hurts so much that you take your revenge on it by calling it names like Nostalgia and Romanticism and Adolescence."[2]

The far-off country, the room called Remember, the

Restaurant of Hope—are all one and the same, and the sense of its presence is woven into our fabric as human beings. We cannot deny its inconsolable whisper to us, yet when we listen and respond, we feel foolhardy and immature. C. S. Lewis said, "We cannot tell it because it is a desire for something that has never actually appeared in our experience. We cannot hide it because our experience is constantly suggesting it, and we betray ourselves like lovers at the mention of a name."[3] Ultimately, every other longing finds its home in the only thing that can expand and change us here—the hope of heaven. Saint Augustine says:

> *Let us sing alleluia here on earth, while we still live in anxiety, so that we may sing it one day in heaven in full security. . . . We shall have no enemies in heaven, we shall never lose a friend. God's praises are sung both there and here, but here they are sung in anxiety, there in security; here they are sung by those destined to die, there, by those destined to live forever; here they are sung in hope, there in hope's fulfillment; here, they are sung by wayfarers, there, by those living in their own country. So then . . . let us sing now, not in order to enjoy a life of leisure, but in order to lighten our labors. You should sing as wayfarers do—sing, but continue your journey. . . . Sing then, but keep going.*[4]

Kathleen Norris says these words by Augustine tempt her to believe that the power to imagine such a heaven is almost heaven enough.[5] Almost. But heaven is out of reach. We know it eludes us, even as we sing. Blaise Pascal says, "We sail within a vast sphere, ever drifting in uncertainty, driven from end to end. When we think to attach ourselves to any point and to fasten to it, it wavers and leaves us; and if we follow it, it eludes our grasp, slips past us, and vanishes forever."[6] But elusive as it is, the manna of knowing each other gives a glimpse of the expanse of heaven, brings its imaginings a little closer to our reach. Brent's life sang a song that compelled me and countless others to imagine heaven. Now he isn't here, so imagination is all his wife, Ginny, and their sons, Drew and Ben, have of him. On many days even the imagination is out of reach.

Brent's life was refined, but it didn't shine with the luster of newly polished silver. It was chiseled and haggard and bore the glory of God in a vessel that resembled an old cowboy coffeepot that had been left on the fire too long. Brent would have turned fifty-one on the day of his funeral, and his face showed his age. His eyes were piercing and brilliant, though, with the joy of a little boy who was just getting to know his father's sense of humor. He was a subtle blend of Clint Eastwood and a person you'd find under the interstate bridge.

Brent was present. Rarely a glance toward the door or a look at the watch, not many glazed looks or superficial nods. Mostly it was questions, more questions, and lots of laughter. Brent was gifted with insight, and somehow he had a view of what God might be up to inside a person's heart. During the last few years of his life, he spoke often of heaven, but he spoke more often of the internal landscape of a person's soul, the terrain that is either captured by the love of Christ or given over to enemy occupation.

Brent knew the sting of betrayal, understood the realities of abandonment, and waged a constant battle with resignation and cynicism. On his most cynical days he infuriated me. Even so, his curiosity penetrated others' hearts, often taking people off guard. One woman tells the story of how offensive he seemed to her on their second encounter because he was inquiring of her life with such penetrating curiosity. After a time, though, she realized she was honored that someone would inquire about the internal realities of her life . . . her thoughts, opinions, struggles, joys. Such curiosity flowed from the landscape of Brent's heart. This world had lost its flavor for Brent; he was already a citizen of heaven. He had little to prove, so he had energy to inquire of others.

A friend recently told me of Kelly Monroe's words describing her sense of loss after the death of her mentor and friend Henri Nouwen: "Some say that loss of love is like the loss of a limb.

You must relearn to function. For me, loss of friendship can feel more like the loss of a vital organ: a heart, or a brain, or lungs. To live through such a loss is to relearn to feel, to move, to think, and to breathe."[7] That comes close to what I and countless others are facing in realizing that Brent is out of reach.

So, what is the way through? How do we walk on this terrain, waiting for our distant country? How do we live limbless, learn to breathe, suffer our losses without somehow efficiently cleaning up our desire to have him back? How do we ache without becoming hardened? I think at this point it's becoming clear, isn't it? We have to surrender.

Surrendering to Kingdom Eyes

When Jesus left His disciples, He spoke to them with a tender understanding of what their journey without Him would be like. Soon He would be out of reach, and they would have to let go of Him, trusting that their surrender was in keeping with the unfolding story He had told them. But the unfolding story wasn't pretty—martyrs' crosses and coliseum jeers. They would be hated as the world hated Jesus. He said His Spirit would come to guide them into all truth, to comfort them, to reveal their foolishness. His friends couldn't take it all in. They didn't really care where He was going; they were just sad because He wouldn't be with them. No wonder He said this to them: "Oh, there is so much more I want to tell you, but you can't bear it now" (John 16:12).

Even when the expanse of heaven is offered to us, it is out of reach to our feeble hearts. No wonder Jesus said to His followers with such frequency, "Take heart." Jesus gives us only what our hearts can handle, even when it is giving Himself. He knows our capacity to receive His love expands each time we remember Him and take heart. There's so much more, He says, but we can't bear it. We can't bear it until we take heart. We can't bear it until our hearts expand. And our hearts expand only as we realize just how out of reach He is. Our loss compels us to cry out. The Spirit responds and expands our hearts. This expansion is a slow one indeed.

WAITING TO BE FOUND

This heart expansion is what was asked of Cora in *The Last of the Mohicans*. Forgive this simplification of the movie based on the novel by James Fenimore Cooper: Hawkeye was the adopted son of Mohican Indians. He had captured Cora's heart, though she was the daughter of an aristocratic British colonel. Now he had to go off to battle. He did not want to leave her behind. Cora and her sister, with Hawkeye and the Mohicans, were being stalked by Magua, the leader of a treacherous tribe. Magua had chased them behind a waterfall, and it was here that Hawkeye had to make his decision. He could stay and make sure Cora was protected, or he could leap through the waterfall in order to get to the greater battle. Cora implored him to go. Hawkeye did not want to leave her, but he knew she was right. His eyes pierced hers as he shouted over the roar of the waterfall, "I will find you. No matter how long it takes, no matter how far, I will find you. You stay alive. As long as one of us is alive, something of the other will remain alive as well. *You stay alive!*"

Cora was being asked to surrender her desires for the greater purposes of the battle, and in doing so, she left herself alone, unsheltered, vulnerable to enemy attack. The only thing she had left was a promise and a plea. She had the promise that she would not be forgotten; Hawkeye would find her. She had the plea to literally stay alive so she could be found. Hawkeye was gone, out of reach, but she had his promise and his plea.

Cora's path is our heart's path every day. We have a promise in our alleyway that we are not forgotten. Our dreams are out of reach. Those we love are out of reach. The love we are looking for is out of reach. But we have the Lord's promise: "I am leaving you with a gift—peace of mind and heart. And the peace I give isn't like the peace the world gives. So don't be troubled or afraid. Remember what I told you: I am going away, but I will come back to you again" (John 14:27-28).

And Jesus puts in His plea this message: "Keep your heart alive so the Spirit I send will find you—He'll comfort you, guide you into all truth, and show you when you wander. Let hope prompt your vision of the day of My return. I am out of reach now, but I will give My Spirit to you as a taste of the day when I will consummate My commitment to you. I will find you, no matter how long it takes."

To be entrusted with what is out of reach—it pulls on our femininity with fervor, doesn't it? We long to give ourselves this way. We long to abandon ourselves to the greater story that is being written for us and for all who are lost. Oh, but how terrifying! We understand May's words, "It is beautiful because it is a homecoming, because it is a liberation from slavery, and because it enables love. But it is fierce because it entails relinquishment, letting go, risking, and enduring losses that are very real and very painful."[8] Even so, we long to worship. We long to lean into the strong shoulders of Jesus—we yearn for His Spirit more than life.

Philip Yancey says, "God holds back; he hides himself; he weeps. Why? Because he desires what power can never win. He is a king who wants not subservience, but love."[9] Our hearts can surrender to that kind of lover, can't they? We have misunderstood the heart of God, misrepresented it—we have believed we must be subservient, so we've been afraid to loosen our grip. But the truth is simple. God will track us down because, as Hawkeye said, if one of us survives, a part of the other one will also. Trust in that kind of covenant allows us to let go.

Getting Lost for a While

This is felt as we send our child out the door to his first day of kindergarten. It is felt as our love for photography has to go into hibernation while our family is developing and our children are pulling at our jeans. It is felt when there is a rift with our husband, and he moves toward us with a desire for sex (we can either deal honestly with our own heart with a view toward the relationship or push the conflict away in denial and go through the motions of lovemaking). Each bittersweet moment when we relinquish ourselves to something bigger and greater than the moment at hand, each time we relax and trust that we will be okay even if we get lost for a while, is worship. The apostle Paul said,

> *This precious treasure—this light and power that now shine within us—is held in perishable containers, that is, in our weak bodies. So everyone can see that our glorious power is from God and is not our own.*
>
> *We are pressed on every side by troubles, but we are not crushed and broken. We are perplexed, but we don't give up and quit. We are hunted down, but God never abandons us. We get knocked down, but we get up again and keep going. Through suffering, these bodies of ours constantly share in the death of Jesus so that the life of Jesus may also be seen in our bodies.* (2 Corinthians 4:7–10)

When a woman gets lost for a while, she understands what His death is.

Robert Bly speaks of a rite of passage for boys conducted by a particular tribe in New Guinea. In this rite, the mothers of eight- to twelve-year-old boys who have lived solely with the women up to this point, wait for the men of the tribe to "invade" and take the boys away. The mothers say nothing to their sons to prepare them for this, and they put on a grand act as the fathers pillage their homes. The boys can be heard yelling, "Mama, save me!" The mothers fight but feign powerlessness and allow the sons to be taken away to a time of training in manhood. Bly writes, "The mothers go home, have coffee, meet the other women and say, 'How did I do?' 'Did I look fierce enough?' 'You were great!'"[10] What a kind gift for a mother to surrender her son to the bigger picture of his life, knowing there is much strength in him to be unleashed! What a contrast to a mother who hovers over her son with concerned worry! This rite is a powerful picture of how a woman can die to her own needs — getting lost for a while — in order to allow another to flourish.

My sister did this with her youngest, Daniel, recently. They were at a swimming pool, and Daniel was on a large float. Carole watched from her chair as two bigger boys got on the float with him and started to jeer at him. Carole aches daily for Daniel's sensitive heart — she is aware that things pierce him more than they do the average kid. She could easily have gone over to the pool and reprimanded the older kids, taking control of the situation and making everything okay for Daniel. But she knew she had to let go.

She waited until later when she could talk to Daniel and hear how it all was for him. He admitted he had been frightened. Carole put her face right up to his, made an angry face, and said, "Daniel, if those kids come back, you do this. Put your face right up to theirs and tell them to get lost!" Daniel left that interaction knowing his mother believed in his strength and ability to handle a situation. Carole left the interaction with a deeper ache than ever. She died to herself for a moment; she let go of control so her son could grow. Oh, but it's costly, isn't it? It requires a deep trust that God will find us, hold our hearts in the process.

SURRENDER WITH DESIRE

Even though the winds of postmodernism have brought a new spiritual awareness, far too often it is an awareness that detaches itself from the yearning of the heart. The rise of interest in Eastern philosophies in the last decade is a case in point.

Buddhism has at its core a call to surrender without desire. Interestingly enough, that comes close to a good definition of the psychological term *disassociation*. So, what does it mean to surrender *with* desire?

Women like my sister and the New Guinea tribal women have become intimately acquainted with what the Hebrews called *kamar* (literally, "a deep yearning" or "shriveling as with heat"). In Hebrew culture the word *kamar* meant the soul had to admit that it was shriveling, deeply affected as it yearned for more. We are led by the hand of Christ into the depths of desire, and there we are asked to relinquish control. To get lost for a while in the midst of *kamar* is simply not possible unless someone bigger than ourselves is holding up our hearts.

SUSPENSE, SEX, AND STILLNESS

Peter Kreeft reminds us, "The French call sexual intercourse *le petit mal,* the little death. It is an end, a consummation, like death, yet a consummation devoutly to be wished. The mystics speak of their desire to die in God, to become nothing in God, everything and nothing, *todo y nada* (Saint John of the Cross)."[11] These yearnings to give ourselves fully—to die in order to experience a moment of what was meant to be—this is the essence of yearning for what is out of reach. Our longing to die, to suffer the loss of self, to relinquish all we hold in our control—this is abandonment to the Spirit. This is worship.

As women, we feel this every hour, not just in bed with someone. We struggle to relax even as someone begins to pursue us in conversation. We wonder how it is possible to let go this much, to let go enough to say, "Okay, you jump through that waterfall. I'll be lost for a while. I'm trembling, but I will be okay. Whatever is going on that is out of reach, whatever the greater purposes are that are unfolding, that is what I want to give myself to. I will trust." It simply isn't possible, this side of the Fall, to trust like that without the Spirit of God. So every time we trust, we worship. Every time we let go, we abandon ourselves to the Spirit's keeping. Every time we relinquish our pettiness in order to bring pleasure to others, we die, let resurrection power have its way, and then we rest.

Think of what it takes to have good sex. Good sex is not possible unless both partners are willing to relinquish their needs for the moment, so that the needs of the other can be fulfilled. Timing is everything. As both people give completely, needs that could never be articulated are mysteriously met. Perhaps you're yawning (or rolling your eyes) as you read this—you've never known such selfless timing. Oh, we are cynical when it comes to sex. I guess that's my point. What it takes for a moment of true ecstasy (being transported to what is out of reach) is death. It takes the hourly, daily death of emotional and spiritual intimacy. We have to die to ourselves, surrender control completely. We have to give ourselves up wholly for the sake of the other. Death gives us a taste of heaven. Relinquishment gives us moments of satisfied stillness.

VISION OF THE REAL

I received the news of Brent's death at 11:00 P.M. on a Saturday. I was in Indiana. I couldn't get a flight back to Colorado until the next day, so I spent twelve long hours waiting, surrounded by friends, as the shock reverberated through me. The next morning I went to church; what else was I to do in my waiting? As the congregation sang their hymns, I was taken somewhere by God—transported—and given a gift. I saw Brent's face. I wasn't *remembering* his face; I was *seeing* his face for the first time. I know it was Brent, but he was more full, more *true*, than I had ever known him before. My thought was *Oh, so that's Brent.*

Sheldon Vanauken speaks of meeting C. S. Lewis for lunch: "We talked, I recall, about death, or rather, awakening after death. Whatever it would be like, we thought, our response to it would be, 'Why, of course it's like this. How else could it have possibly been?'"[12] This is why we can't hold on to the things and the people that give us joy here on earth. Friendship, love, intimacy, ecstasy—it's all a shadow of the true "of course" things that are coming. Oh, we try. I try to make my relationships, the sunshine on my petunias, the thrill of skiing powder, the joy I know in walking with people the true thing. I have to drink in these things to keep desire alive, right? But then I have to let go. C. S. Lewis said,

> These things—the beauty, the memory of our own past—are good images of what we really desire; but if they are mistaken for the thing itself, they turn into dumb idols, breaking the hearts of their worshipers. For they are not the thing itself; they are only the scent of a flower we have not found, the echo of a tune we have not heard, news from a country we have never yet visited.[13]

A SERVANT LORD

Jesus came to us in the fullness of time (Galatians 4:4) and took the form of a servant (Philippians 2:7). The role He chose to take for us is that of a *doulos*, a slave, one given up wholly for another's will. The relinquishment He knew is beyond our comprehension, and He did it for us not only to meet our need for redemption but also to know us. To have us back. To take our hand and show us what true intimacy is.

He surrendered His needs as He wandered about with no place to call home. He surrendered fully to the purposes of His Father, not without Gesthemane resistance, but nevertheless fully. He surrendered His reputation though He knew His name was King of kings and Lord of lords. He did not consider equality with God a thing to be grasped (Philippians 2:6), so He held back as thorns were crushed into His skull, knowing that His stripes were going to heal us. He shed blood to fulfill the law of love on our behalf. He emptied Himself— *todo y nada*—just to have our hearts. George MacDonald wrote in a letter, "When we are all just as loving and unselfish as Jesus; when like him, our one thought of delight is that God is, and is what he is; when the fact that a being is just another person from ourselves, is enough to make that being precious—then, darling, you and I and all will have the grand liberty wherewith Christ makes free."[14] Sharon Hersh puts it this way:

> That God invites harlots to intimacy is almost beyond compre-
> hension. That he desperately hungers for intimacy is an ineffable
> mystery that somehow intersects with human stories of love
> sought, love lost, and love endured. The revelation of God's des-
> perate love compels us to consider that he is simply in love with
> us more than our mind is capable of reconciling with the way we
> still have to think of God.[15]

KNOWING AND BEING KNOWN

Looking ahead with yearning to the day when all things would be revealed to him in heaven, the apostle Paul affirmed, "Then I shall know fully, even as I am fully known" (1 Corinthians 13:12, NIV). Here is a yearning that all followers of Jesus can resonate with, and an affirmation we can echo. Yet we know that in this life there is always more to know.

Conduct an experiment with yourself. Every time you think, hear, or read about knowing or being known by God, push the envelope to think of the union between a husband and a wife: *le petit mal.* You go on a trip with your husband to a beach cabin and have a wonderful intimate time—you know each other in the sexual sense as the waves pound the coastline. Does this mean that you now know him completely? Hardly. There's always more, isn't there? As C. S. Lewis said, "A man may love a woman and not win her; but it would be very odd if the phenomenon called 'falling in love' occurred in a sexless world."[16]

Somehow a truly intimate time serves only to remind us that there's something beyond us, so much more to know. M. Scott Peck believed "spiritual and sexual desires are so closely intertwined that you cannot arouse one without the other."[17] There is always more spiritual and emotional intimacy to know.

This is where I am grateful to be writing to women. Women are more comfortable with the imagery of being Christ's bride than men are, and understandably so. But we also carry with us the sting of abuse, betrayal, and all those times our vulnerability has been assaulted. We have much to deal with in our hearts before our time at the beach can be pleasurable. And God has much to show us about what is in our hearts toward Him before we can fully know Him.

When you get to heaven, will you know Jesus? The apostle John said we will be like Him, for we will see Him as He is (1 John 3:2). The apostle Paul said we will know Him even as we are fully known (1 Corinthians 13:12). Will it be like the beach? Will we be intimate, left wanting for more of Him? Will we live in freedom, the complete rest of knowing that we have eternity to discover Him? To explore? To finally embark on the adventure we've been envisioning? There will be no convincing us that there is more outside of Jesus; there will instead be an ongoing understanding that there is always more *in* Him. As T. S. Eliot wrote,

And the end of all our exploring
Will be to arrive where we started
And know the place for the first time.[18]

When I was a young Presbyterian girl watching a wedding, I lost my breath when the couple said to each other, "With my body I thee worship." Gasp! I couldn't believe such things were talked about within the walls of a church, let alone proclaimed as part of the wedding service. These words seemed to make the whole sanctuary hush for a moment. I learned they were sacred words. I'm still learning just *how* sacred. The worship committed to in these vows is a covenant to put aside all that gets in the way of true intimacy, to enter into a sacred place of knowing the other that opens the heart's doors to all that is out of reach. This mystery, Paul told us, is "an illustration of the way Christ and the church are one" (Ephesians 5:32).

Jesus relinquished everything to have our hearts. Mocked and beaten, He did it. On the long road to the Place of the Skull (Calvary, Golgotha), He did it. Pierced in the side, blood streaming from thorns penetrating His scalp, He did it. Jesus relinquished His needs, His very life, to make us glorious. Responding to this sacred love calls us out of our deepest desire, calls us to die to self in order to worship Him. George MacDonald said, "There is nothing good but being one with him in every desire and hope and joy."[19] John Piper echoes this, "God's pursuit of praise from us and our pursuit of pleasure in him are one and the same pursuit. God's quest to be glorified and our quest to be satisfied reach their goal in this one experience: our delight in God which overflows in praise."[20] Knowing Jesus here — worshiping Him — is preparing us for more of Him in heaven. Carolyn Arends captures how thirsty we will be until heaven, in her song "Reaching":

> We are reaching for the future, we are reaching for the past
> And no matter what we have we reach for more.
> We are desperate to discover what is just beyond our grasp
> Maybe that's what heaven is for.
> Still it seems a tragic fate, living with the quiet ache,
> the constant strain
> for what remains just out of reach.
> So when we taste of the Divine, it leaves us thirsty every time
> For one more taste of what awaits when heaven's gates are reached.

SEPARATED FOR NOW

Now that Brent is gone, those of us who loved him miss all we knew of him, and we're painfully aware of all of him that we never got a chance to experience. So it goes with intimacy. We know each other, but then we realize all the ways we are separated, the ways we hold back, the ways we hide from and hurt each other. And then we thirst for more. Again, it's the thirst for more that expands our hearts. I am more than furious as I write these words because I know Ginny would do anything to have Brent back rather than have an expanding heart. Of course she would. It's a huge problem for her and for all of us. But it goes back to how we are convinced.

The movie *What Dreams May Come* is a visually beautiful, provocative film. I was deeply disturbed by it. There was so much about this movie to like in terms of the sheer color and vibrancy brought to the image of heaven. But the essence of *this* heaven was the soul-mate relationship between the man and the woman, created over and over again by them. Does this reflect the eternal themes of innocence, crisis, threat, danger, and victory? It comes close but never gets there.

Obviously, through the centuries, good literature has repre-sented evil as something that gets in the way of love. The hero battles this force and captures the heroine at all costs. The theme is about the hero defeating evil for the sake of the heroine. In this movie there is no evil. There is nothing to defeat except separation, so everything is ultimately up to us—a pursuit to find each other. In this movie love is about us, but it is up to us to close the gap to create the power to find each other. Love will be beautiful if we just give ourselves to its creation. There is nothing out of reach to our fertile imaginings. How reflective of the direction our culture is moving, but more, how reflective of the original deceit: "You can have more if you just take a bite and believe you are worthy of—no, *above*—the knowledge of good and evil." How seductive! We have no need of mercy to obtain this heaven. We don't need to wait. Go after the "more"; it is yours. How exhausting!

Similarly, Aldous Huxley's portrayal of "a streamlined, soulless Eden" in *Brave New World* is an example of what happens when there is nothing out of reach — no resistance, no suffering, no loss. "Everybody is happy now" is the central theme. There is no Monet, no Chopin, no O'Keefe. There is no suffering, so there is no beauty. Kreeft says of it,

> *Motherhood, childbirth, and families are regarded as obscene and inefficient. The sources of suffering are all dried up. The characters are happy because they are part puppet, part animal, and part vegetable. The only human character, John, the savage from an Indian reservation, can maintain his humanity and his sanity only by suffering and death, and since his brave new world gives him no opportunity for either, he is driven to self-flagellation and finally suicide.* [21]

Our separation is the problem. But our separation comes from death. George MacDonald wrote, "We are all just children in our Father's nursery. Some of us are taken before others away from it, and we are left without our playmates."[22] Only a cruel enemy could be responsible for such a thing. Death entered as Eve was convinced there was more apart from trusting God's care, and Adam stood idly by. Death is the birthplace of all suffering and angst. Without death, we have no need for hope. It was Jesus' mission, after all, to steal back the keys of sin and death. Jesus takes away death's sting, but death is still the enemy. I do not know what to do with Brent's death. It has stolen one of the finest gems from the earth. Concerning the death of his son, Nicholas Wolterstorff has written:

> *When the writer of Revelation spoke of the coming day of shalom, he did not say that on that day we would live at peace with death. He said that on that day ". . . there will be no more death or*

mourning or crying or pain, for the old order of things has passed away." I shall try to keep the wound from healing, in recognition of our living still in the old order of things. I shall try to keep it from healing, in solidarity with those who sit beside me on humanity's mourning beach.[23]

Some wounds were not meant to be entirely healed here on earth. Sometimes the wounds are all we have to remind us of the one we love. George MacDonald said:

I think we shall talk of all the old times with the hearts of divinely glad little ones — and sometimes wonder that we made such a work about certain things. We shall have everything, for the father who loves us, and is himself, as Dante calls him, "the glad creator," will see that his dear little ones are happy indeed, and have all they want. It will be safe then to give us all we want, for we shall not forget him, or forget that he gives us EVERYTHING.[24]

But those conversations aren't here yet. Here we have wounds and lost limbs and desire and thirst. And Saint Augustine's call to "sing then, but keep going." The call to surrender to all that is out of reach.

8

OUR LOVER'S EYES

*"But then I will win her back once again.
I will lead her out into the desert and speak
tenderly to her there. I will return her vineyards
to her and transform the Valley of Trouble (theValley
of Achor) into a gateway of hope. She will give herself to
me there, as she did long ago when she was young. . . ."*

The Valley of Achor must have been a dreadful place. Its name
literally means "the Valley of Suffering, or Trouble." If you have
driven through Death Valley or certain regions of southern New
Mexico or Arizona, you have some idea of *stark nothingness*.
There is nothing there that would prompt any vision—nothing
to look forward to. So why would God choose such a place,
such barren terrain, to be called "the door of hope"?

A woman I respect has a deep, rich beauty in her soul. This
beauty has grown in her through a dark season, a private journey through her own wilderness. Widowed with grown children, she developed a close friendship with a man she met at
work. What she felt in response to him caught her off guard.
Over the course of years, she had become stale. She wasn't
unhappy—she was simply deflated—aware of a growing ache.

139

If someone had told her it was unmet desire she would have initially scoffed but secretly would have thought, *Well, I am feeling pretty lonely these days.* This new friend shared her love of music and of the waters of the Chesapeake in ways that had always seemed forced with her other friends. He was a sensitive man and could draw out her heart in a natural way; in the way she always longed for. He was compelling, passionate, and frequently encouraged her in her gifts and abilities. This man was also deeply and profoundly committed to his wife. There was little question that his heart was completely devoted to his spouse and family. Occasionally she thought she felt his movement toward her as more than platonic. She just couldn't tell. But the presence of this man forced her to remember who she was—who that winsome little girl was, what the passionate woman desired. Now the pivotal question . . . what would she do with all that was being stirred within her?

THE DARK THRESHOLD

This is where she entered the dark threshold of her soul's hope. This woman had the integrity to know that, although everything good was stirred in her through this man's presence in her life, she did not want to bring damage to his marriage, nor to his family. As she confronted her own heart, listening to the desire that was being stirred instead of running from it, she was compelled to deal with her own heart. She faced that she had hidden her true desires for years. She had ceased offering herself to others for fear that her desires would never be met anyway. Coming to terms with what she desired—asking for it and then surrendering her heart in the midst of her disappointment—was a difficult challenge. But she allowed herself to see she couldn't love well without this ongoing process.

She held what had been stirred within her in a completely private, lonely place. "It was a silent place," she said, "a place no one else knew about, even the confidantes who knew my struggle with him." It was in this place, this dark and lonely threshold, that she cried out to God in ways she never knew possible. She brought to Him her loneliness, desperation, and desire to be seen and pursued. She brought her envy over how another woman was receiving what she longed for; what she could only taste. She brought the deep ache she felt, and her temptation to just give up and surrender to fantasies or soliciting an affair.

She brought her heart.

And no one knew.

No one but Jesus. He met her there. He tracked her down in that dark place. Many nights were spent in silence. Many hours of many lonely days were spent hearing nothing from Him. But He found her. He allured her into the wilderness, and there He spoke kindly to her. She could have easily chosen to flee God's invitation — there was a man who probably would respond to her advances if she revealed her heart. She could have drawn him out and found some solace in his arms. But she wanted *more*. Kathleen Norris says, "God will find a way to let us know that he is with us *in this place*, wherever we are, however far we think we've run."[1]

This woman honestly faced her desire, didn't flee from it, but allowed God to find her there. And what she wanted opened her heart to a level of suffering she never bargained for. This lonely darkness brought a level of intimacy with Christ she could never conceive of. Faithfulness and courage have breathed new life into her, and for that she is grateful. Her deepest longings are still unmet (as they are for every woman). Yet now she is more stunning than ever.

HIS EYES

What does this woman know that keeps her from fleeing the desire of her own heart into the arms of her married friend? There is something stronger than mere Christian principles holding up this woman's heart. As Sharon Hersh aptly says,

"The traditional catechisms suggesting man is created to know, love and serve God are incomplete. Men and women must also know how much God yearns to love and serve them."[2] And she knows what Albert Schweitzer spoke of when he said, "He will reveal Himself in the toils, the conflicts, the sufferings which they shall pass through in His fellowship, and, as an ineffable mystery, they shall learn in their own experience who He is."[3] She knows Jesus yearns for her, and she longs to get a greater glimpse of His eyes.

First Peter 1:3-8 gives a beautiful description of what Jesus knows to be true about her, and us, in the alleyway:

> *"All honor to the God and Father of our Lord Jesus Christ, for it is by his boundless mercy that God has given us the privilege of being born again. Now we live with a wonderful expectation because Jesus Christ rose again from the dead. For God has reserved a priceless inheritance for his children. It is kept in heaven for you, pure and undefiled, beyond the reach of change and decay. And God, in his mighty power, will protect you until you receive this salvation, because you are trusting him. It will be revealed on the last day for all to see. So be truly glad! There is wonderful joy ahead, even though it is necessary for you to endure many trials for a while. These trials are only to test your faith, to show that it is strong and pure."*

Johannes Tauler says, "God allows our soul to be hard pressed, till there is no other path open to it, but permits this, so that the drink which quenches our thirst may taste all the sweeter and more delicate, now and throughout eternity."[4] Jesus knows our love for Him is ultimately stronger than our other loves. He doesn't take us into the wilderness to see "if we have what it takes." He allures us into the wilderness to *reveal to us what is truly in our hearts* — a strong and pure faith in His love. Oh, He reveals the prodigal, wandering, foolish heart. But He also reveals the deepest heart — our desire for Him. He takes us there to remind us of the love we have for Him. First Peter goes on to say,

> [Your faith] is being tested as fire tests and purifies gold—and your faith is far more precious to God than mere gold. So if your faith remains strong after being tried by fiery trials, it will bring you much praise and glory and honor on the day when Jesus Christ is revealed to the whole world.

> You love him even though you have never seen him. Though you do not see him, you trust him; and even now you are happy with a glorious, inexpressible joy. (1:7–8, emphasis added)

LOOKING INTO HIS EYES

We can't *see* Jesus in the alleyway. But if our hearts are open, I believe we can *glimpse* His eyes.

In the days following my broken engagement, I predictably couldn't shake my fiancé's eyes from my memory. They are deep and clear eyes, eyes that had held such light for me. The eyes are the window to the soul; his eyes mirrored a noble and passionate soul, touched by God. I wished for the image of his eyes to go away—not out of contempt, just out of needing relief. If I could just banish those eyes from my memory, then the loss would be lessened and I could function.

God visited me there. He didn't ask me to remove my love's eyes from my heart, nor did He chide me for trying to banish his memory. He knew it was just too much for me. So He gave me a vision. The vision was of Jesus waiting for me at the end of an aisle more beautiful than that of any European cathedral. When I arrived and looked in His eyes, I saw the same light I had seen in my love's eyes, only perfected and true. I realized at that moment that the light I had loved in my fiancé's eyes had been Jesus all along. Did I love this man? Oh, yes, no question.

But Jesus was showing me that what I most needed, what I thought I had lost, was still with me. The vision continued with feasting and festivities celebrating our love. It surpassed anything I could imagine. I had a glimpse of finally knowing Him. I knew then that it was true:

> No eye has seen, no ear has heard,
> and no mind has imagined
> what God has prepared
> for those who love him. (1 Corinthians 2:9)

THE DOOR OF HOPE

A God who meets us in betrothal—*that* God we can handle. But what are we to do with a God who chooses one of His prophets and says to him, "Go and marry a prostitute, so some of her children will be born to you from other men" (Hosea 1:2)? This God wants to illustrate how far we've strayed from our truest heart, how we have openly committed adultery by worshiping other gods. Hosea had the rare privilege of experiencing what God experiences each moment in relationship with us.

Hosea marries Gomer. We are not told much about this prostitute, but we are told much by the names given to her children. The name of Lo-ruhamah, a daughter of Gomer, means "not loved." "For," says God, "I will no longer show love to the people of Israel or forgive them" (Hosea 1:6). The name of Lo-ammi, a son, means "not my people." "For Israel is not my people, and I am not their God" (verse 9). And we are told that Gomer is a picture of us. God's broken heart is heard as He says harshly,

> "But now, call Israel to account, for she is no longer my wife,
> and I am no longer her husband. Tell her to take off her garish
> makeup and suggestive clothing and to stop playing the prostitute.

*If she doesn't, I will strip her naked as she was on the day she
was born. I will leave her to die of thirst, as in a desert or a
dry and barren wilderness. And I will not love her children
as I would my own because they are not my children! They
were conceived in adultery. For their mother is a shameless
prostitute and became pregnant in a shameful way. She said,
'I'll run after other lovers and sell myself to them for food
and drink, for clothing of wool and linen, and for olive oil.'"*
(Hosea 2:1–5)

We all live Gomer's story. I never knew how much I allowed
my vision of marriage to become my other lover. Over the years
I have crafted a secret place inside my heart, a vision of marriage
where I am completely cared for and never failed. It is born out
of a legitimate desire, just as Gomer's desire for love was legitimate. But just as she took her desire and squandered it with
lovers who could never satisfy her, so I have made this secret
fantasy a place I flee into instead of bringing my longings and
fears to God's heart. You can imagine, then, that when my
engagement ended it did not just hold the pain of lost love; it
held an internal shriek. I was being stripped. I was naked before
God, and my other lover was in full view.

God says of Gomer,

*"But I will fence her in with thornbushes. I will block the road to
make her lose her way. When she runs after her lovers, she won't
be able to catch up with them. She will search for them but not
find them. Then she will think, 'I might as well return to my husband because I was better off with him than I am now.' She doesn't
realize that it was I who gave her everything she has — the grain,
the wine, the olive oil."* (Hosea 2:6–8)

Those months had been that for me. I was fenced in. I had
lost my way. Slowly I began to understand that what I desired in
my fantasy was already with me. Slowly I understood how my

betrayal broke Jesus' heart. He cared for me all along. God gives this hopeful promise:

> *"But then I will win her back once again. I will lead her out into the desert and speak tenderly to her there. I will return her vineyards to her and transform the Valley of Trouble into a gateway of hope.* She will give herself to me there, *as she did long ago when she was young, when I freed her from her captivity."* (Hosea 2:14–15, emphasis added)

As Jesus spoke to me in that desert, the desire of my fantasy was purified. My desire actually deepened. I longed for marriage more than ever before. But in the wilderness I gave myself to Jesus, which meant giving Him my desire. He freed me from the captivity of my fantasy and gave me the pure desire of a lonely woman. But now I want to run to Him with that desire—there is nowhere else to go!

Gomer's story is our story. Hosea 6 is the culmination of this promise—the rains of spring come after a long, dusty time in Achor. After being led out into the wilderness, exposed in her adultery, Israel is led by God to this place. The Lord has torn her to pieces, and now He will heal her. We are led out, sometimes under siege, to a place where we must acknowledge our wounds. Only as we feel His breath—first frightening, then kind—do we realize the wounds have been inflicted in His tender discipline, in a severe wooing of our souls.

FOUND BY GOD

God fences us in. He destroys the vineyards we create to satisfy ourselves. He then takes us to that dark place where the only way out is to be found. We discover that we cannot move, and in so doing we are surprised with how much we were meant to be still. We discover we have expended useless energy in coming up with our own provisions, and we are caught off guard with how *enough* He is. "Notice that in the Gospels there is never, unless I am mistaken," says Simone Weil, "question of a search for God by man. In all the parables it is the Christ who seeks men. . . . Or again, a man finds the Kingdom of God as if by chance, and then, but only then, he sells all."[5] We must be found by God in our adultery. And we must be found by God in our desire for Him.

We do not come to fully understand our desire until we are fenced in, in the wilderness, by the lover of our soul. It is in this place, He says, that "you will call me 'my husband' instead of 'my master.'

> "O Israel, I will cause you to forget your images of Baal; even their names will no longer be spoken. . . . I will make you my wife forever, showing you righteousness and justice, unfailing love and compassion. I will be faithful to you and make you mine, and you will finally know me as LORD." (Hosea 2:16–17,19–20, emphasis added)

SUDDEN INTRUSIONS

The alleyway is a very personal place, a place only our hearts know. And only our hearts know just how hidden God seems to us in the alley, just how much we are asked to continue to live, to journey through Achor, waiting in expectation for that sudden intrusion into the darkness. Ambrose, Saint Augustine's mentor, said,

> Take note . . . that the angel appeared suddenly, so that Zechariah was startled. The holy scriptures so often describe angelic and divine appearances as "sudden," and I believe there is a reason why this is so. It is because He wants to reveal with impact some new aspect of His plan or His nature. So in every sense of the word, that which was not seen or perceived before is suddenly revealed—and never to be forgotten.[6]

Along these same lines, Craig Barnes says, "Whenever God sends a messenger with good news for us, it usually means a complete abandonment of the life into which we have settled."[7] Augustine echoed this thought, "We must always keep in mind that it is part of God's very nature to remain unseen—to keep both his will and his nature hidden from human perception—until it is in his perfect will to reveal himself to us."[8] He does reveal His heart and His eyes, and when He does, it is a beautiful intrusion that keeps us alive in the alleyway.

Once, in the Philippines, when I was severely ill with dengue fever, a Filipino friend stood in the corner of the room and began singing. His voice started out soft but soon grew in passionate volume as he bellowed in crystal-clear tenor glory, "His eye is on the sparrow." Tears were streaming down his face. I was delirious, but through the fog I could see that this man loved me and wanted God to tend to me. His plea on my behalf washed over me. It took nearly a year to fully recover from dengue fever, but I have yet to recover from the piercing surprise of Pastor Dalisay's song.

My friend Karen's daughter Kaeli, in the sullen and silent line of the post office, suddenly began to sing "Jesus Loves Me." She was unabashed. She didn't hum or mumble—she sang at the top of her lungs! People slowly started to smile, to turn her way. Soon there were conversations between patrons in line; the entire mood of the dreary post office had changed. It was the power of a beautiful intrusion.

TRANSFORMED BY BEAUTY

These intrusions come into our alleyways to change us, silence us. There's nothing we can do about them—they show up, and we either receive them or ignore them. They are meant to inspire our vision of how to intrude into others' alleyways for the sake of redemption.

We are treated to a glorious intrusion in the movie *Babette's*

Feast. Babette, a French chef, has found herself amid a community of people devoted to barren piety and labor. Circumstances have thrown her onto this shore of Denmark, where there is a sense that these people recently landed here, and going nowhere, they have just made the best of it. There is no color to their homes, no vibrancy to their eyes, no pulse to their relationships. All is deadened and orderly, with an undercurrent of fear — the fear of stepping outside the lines with each other and with God.

Babette takes employment as a cook in one of the homes. Given meager produce and meats to work with, we see her spark start to die down as her creativity and passion are stifled. She must be utilitarian in the very context where she once was free and expressive. Soon a surprise comes from another land. Babette learns that she has won the lottery in France. Our minds race to her freedom; she can now leave this stark prison and return to the place of music, wine, art, and creativity. But she doesn't leave. She sends a long list by courier to France, requesting the ingredients for a lavish meal. An all-day, extravagant meal that costs her everything she has.

Slowly the provisions begin to arrive. Cornish hens quacking in their crates. Choice wines. Seasonings. As the meats and cheeses arrive, Babette smells them with delight. Exotic vegetables and herbs, fruits of every color arrive. Babette's desire is to make a lavish meal for the entire community before she leaves. They tentatively agree, looking askance at the provisions that seem so frivolous to them.

The labor of love takes days to accomplish. The guests are seated, more than uncomfortable. Stiff and stoic, they are not sure how to handle the beauty of the table, the pleasing scent of the appetizers. They hold their wine with uncertainty, knowing its value, and not sure it belongs in their hands. As the beauty unfolds, so does the truth. Brothers who have been walled apart by bitterness begin to soften toward one another. Conversations begin. There is laughter. It is all tenuous, but the breaking-down process is obvious, and they humble themselves to partake of and enjoy this fine affair. Babette is in the kitchen, working hard with an artist's sweat on her brow, pausing for a drink of wine as she smiles, knowing what is naturally occurring in the next room. Beauty is changing everything. Desire is finding these hardened souls, and the intrusion is transforming them.

Don't we want to respond to the stark alleyway with Babette's heart? To lavish everything we know of beauty on the people around us? Jesus did that, of course. Having lost everything in His passionate *doulos* ministry, He lavished the most extravagant gift on the ones who were oblivious to the richness of what He had to offer. Some saw a glimpse of His artistry. Sometimes we see it too. But mostly we just watch with indifference. He fills plates with songs during sickness and in post offices; He brings an unexpected sunrise, a spontaneous call from a friend, a smile in Wal-Mart. He gives us constant reminders of His love for us. But we turn up our noses, thinking, *I'd really rather not eat out here, thank you. If I can't have the full meal, I don't want to be reminded.* Macrina Wiederkehr says we stand in the midst of nourishment, and we starve.[9] In the face of this disregard, God sends Himself in the form of His Son. He gives away His inheritance, lavishing His beauty on our prodigal hearts. In the middle of our chosen forgetfulness, He fulfills the promise given:

> *"But this is what the Lord, the God of Israel says: I will surely bring my people back again from all the countries where I will scatter them in my fury. I will bring them back to this very city and let them live in peace and safety. They will be my people, and I will be their God. And I will give them one heart and mind to worship me forever, for their own good and for the good of all their descendants.*
>
> *"And I will make an everlasting covenant with them. . . . I will* put a desire in their hearts to worship me, *and they will never leave me."* (Jeremiah 32:36–40, emphasis added)

God intrudes and stirs our desire to the point of worship. Jesus displayed this in the Garden of Gethsemane as His desire was stirred through streams of blood and sweat. There He surrendered to His deepest desire: to endure the cross, despising the shame, for the joy set before Him (Hebrews 12:2). *We are His joy.* We are too fearful and proud to be lavished upon, until He reveals our truest heart.

Yes, God reveals our darkness, but even more, He reveals how much we want to trust Him and exactly what we need to ask of Him. Kathleen Norris says, "Darkness is as nothing to God, who can look right through whatever evil we've done in our lives to the creature made in the divine image. I suspect that only God, and well-loved infants, can see this way."[10]

Beauty intrudes to reveal our truest heart. Our truest heart longs to be restored. Our truest heart longs to worship. Our truest heart longs for us to be clothed in the garments of hope, to be compassionate, courageous, and tender women as we persevere in our waiting.

9

HOPE'S ATTIRE

Until we learn to sit at one another's feet,
we will starve at our lavish banquet tables.
—MACRINA WIEDERKEHR

What monarch would have
servants with filthy hands serve his tables?
—CHARLES SPURGEON

Lord, save us from Your followers
—BUMPER STICKER

In the nakedness of the alleyway, what are the garments of hope? The feeble counterfeits sure show themselves, don't they? Eve bore glory, but soon she was clothed in the fig leaf of shame. The Pharisees put on elaborate garments to display their righteousness, all the while blinded to their own internal deadness. The apostle Paul chided the Galatian churches for adding heavy garments of slavery onto the garments of the hope found in salvation through faith in Christ alone. We either remember God's goodness and display hope, or else we forget His goodness and display something false.

The contemporary false version of hope can be seen in the rational clothing with which the church "adorns" herself. Programs, steps, outlines, formulas, advice—these rational rags hang pitifully on a body intended to wear the exquisite garments of hope. This subtle counterfeit entices us with the false promise that our involvement and activity can bring us the life we hope for. Order, discipline, and involvement become the goal. They become garments unto themselves, goals to be mastered with a heart that says, "This is what defines me, and I must accomplish it well." We no longer live from the hope of glory (Christ in us) but from a hope set on our prowess to be great Christians. An odor of staleness fills our lives as the object of our longing becomes our proficiency, our commitment, our stand on various political and moral issues, rather than a yearning for Christ Himself.

We move from the prophet's cry:

Is anyone thirsty? Come and drink—even if you have no money! Come, take your choice of wine or milk—it's all free! Why spend your money on food that does not give you strength? Why pay for food that does you no good? Listen, and I will tell you where to get food that is good for the soul! (Isaiah 55:1–2)

to our pitiful whimper:

Come on in and join us as we work really hard to come up with a consistent perspective on life. We're not really very thirsty; we're too busy to notice if we are, anyway. If you'd like to provide a meal for yourself while you work with us, that would be great— that's what most of us have done, brought a bag lunch. Thanks for coming, and don't forget to sign the guest register.

Hopeful garments are saturated in desperation, not Christian proficiency. David Henderson writes, "One day Existence will speak its last line, take a bow, and draw the curtains. Jesus will come back, and when He does, our upside-down world will be up-ended and restored once and for all. He will do away with evil, craft a new heaven and earth, and make us fully human for the first time."[1]

When existence speaks its last line, polished people won't have much need to celebrate their place at the feast. But those who have been waiting with the groaning of all humanity, desperate from their deep desire to finally be released from all of the false garments, will be speechless that a place is set for them, that God would dine with the human heart that wandered far from home. As we wait in the alleyway, we wear our hopeful humanity through the compassion we show, the tenderness and courage we display in our perseverance, and the loveliness we wear as we are touched by God's mercy in our wandering.

COMPASSION: THE MEMORY OF SPLENDOR

I adore weddings. There is a splendor to even the simplest of wedding ceremonies, and little else can cause me to be caught up in the beauty of what this sacrament points toward: the betrothal and commitment of the Bridegroom and His bride. But I've attended enough weddings to know that I also dread them. There is no mistaking the strange feeling that gnaws at my heart when the wedding party has driven away: It's over. The splendor is gone. And now they—and we—must go about daily living.

Was the splendor a farce? No, it was real. Even the most cynical eyes or concerned relatives cannot dismiss it. This is why my post-wedding angst persists: I don't want the splendor to end. Especially the look in the bridegroom's eyes. It may seem strange, but in a way this missing-the-splendor reaction comes close to defining biblical compassion.

Compassion is called out of us when we see situations where there is an obvious absence of something or someone life-giving. It calls us to ache, mostly because we are forced to long for the restoration of whatever or whoever is absent. For those of us who have tasted the riches of Christ, compassion calls us to want to extend His heart into the situation, to be ministers of reconciliation and restoration. Of course, we can choose to enter these situations with nothing more than a haughty, sacrificial stance in which we say to ourselves, *It sure is a good thing I am here helping out. And now that I think about it, I'm an amazing and wonderful person for giving up my time and energy to be here.* This stance, this path of least resistance that I know so well, focuses only on what we have to give—not on what we desire to have restored.

We are told to go and learn what it means that God desires compassion more than sacrifice (Matthew 9:13). Jesus gives us these words in the context of showing us His heart for eating with tax gatherers and sinners—a context for exposing the hard hearts of all of us who wish to fast in order to be seen by others. Any fast that matters, He says, involves mourning. And His followers, He says, won't mourn until He is gone from their presence. When He, the Bridegroom, is taken away, then they will mourn and fast.

Now, when the bride and bridegroom drive away from us—when our taste of splendor ends—we are left with the banal reality of our lives. We are left with the poverty of our own condition. We are left to live, nourished only by a memory of the splendor that once was. Sacrificial living requires nothing of our hearts because it has no sight, no memory, no vision. Compassion requires us to see what is gone, to remember what was, and to long for those things and those people to be restored. Compassion is being broken over how little we grieve the absence of Christ in our lives.

INTERNAL POVERTY

Never has my definition of compassion been challenged so much as during the years when I had the privilege of living and working in southern Africa. In an era when the vestiges of apartheid were crumbling, it was an electric place, an exhilarating time to walk the soil of that beautiful continent. It was a land of contrasts, yet a similar pulse beat through the homes of the wealthy plantation owners and businesspeople as beat through the stench-ridden, crowded slums of the townships.

It was in one of these townships, in a simple home of a displaced Mozambican family, that I met a boy named Musa. Musa looked about six when his piercing brown eyes caught mine. He had one of those grins that seemed to spread across his entire face. I found myself filled with delight at this little boy. What I didn't realize as I made faces with Musa was that he was actually twelve years old and had been mute for almost six years and could no longer walk, or even stand, on his own. A debilitating muscular disease, his mother told me, as she pulled him from a small washbasin outside their stucco home. My heart was filled with what I thought was compassion.

Compelled by this family, I found myself spending quite a bit of time in their home. I looked on as Musa's mother, Ketsiwe, discovered the love of Christ with a zeal I have rarely seen since. She began urgently knocking on little wooden doors to tell her neighbors what she had come to realize about the love of God. Pretty soon there was a humble living room filled with kerchiefed African women (and an occasional man) desiring to search the Scriptures together. The *inyanga* (witch doctor) next door curiously relented in her threats to destroy such meetings and eventually joined the inquisitive crowd.

These thirsty and curious ones decided they needed to pray for Musa. And they did—fervently. One day, while we all watched in disbelief, Musa took his mother's hand and stood up. He let go of her hand, took several shaky steps, and then collapsed. With his first words in six years, he mumbled, *"Siabonga, Jesu"* ("Thank you, Jesus"). He again got up and feebly made his way around the small house. An incredible wail came from my African friends. Musa was walking. Musa was talking. Prayer had been heard, and the answer was a scene of absolute wonder.

I held that day—and that little boy—in my heart as a picture of what is possible. The image of that big-grinned, twisted little boy gaining strength was one I drew upon whenever I felt the futility of life and faith creeping into my heart. I returned to the United States with my heart captured by Musa and by the unlimited power of God. And sadly, I held it as a picture that no longer prompted compassion. After all, Musa's "plight" was lessened now, right?

A year and a half later, I had the opportunity to return to southern Africa for several weeks. The first stop was predictable; I had to visit Ketsiwe and Musa. I expectantly worked my way down the muddy slope to Musa's home, only to find that there was no one in the house. As I turned the corner into the back garden, I felt the life drain out of me as I saw Ketsiwe washing Musa in a basin again. He was more emaciated and twisted than ever. He had taken a bad turn for the worse in the past five months, Ketsiwe told me. Musa could speak, and he greeted me. His eyes embraced me as I wept and internally raged at God. *What a cruel joke,* I thought—*to have a taste of life and freedom and then to be subjected again to this miserable existence!* The splendor I had witnessed was gone, and I was furious.

Then Musa and I spent the day together, and the little teenager completely silenced me. All he wanted to talk about, from his borrowed wheelchair, were me, Jesus, and his friends. He occasionally sang out, thanking God that we were together. He wanted to pray with me. He was absolutely in love with Christ, and it permeated his every breath. He told me about the church that had started in his neighborhood—started because so many people had heard about him, he said.

I had nothing to say. The "compassion" I had thought I'd had for Musa was revealed as nothing more than a convenient way to avoid the utter sadness of his situation (and mine). But it was not his condition that drew me to true compassion. It was his heart—his glorious, splendor-filled heart. The petty complaints of my soul were exposed, and when I looked at this boy, I decided to learn all I could from him in our hours together. Through him I saw the poverty of my own arrogant, "sacrificial" love. I have never been the same.

THE POVERTY OF THE BRIDEGROOM'S ABSENCE

Father Zossima, in Dostoyevsky's *The Brothers Karamazov,* points to the yearning of compassion when he proclaimed:

God took seeds from other worlds and sowed them on this earth and made his garden grow, and everything that could come up came up, but whatever grows is alive and lives only through the feeling of its contact with other mysterious worlds: if that feeling grows weak or is destroyed in you then what has grown up in you will also die. Then you will become indifferent to life and even grow to hate it. [2]

How do we extend our hearts in a society that is enamored with therapeutic prowess and in a church that is anemic, lacking the nutrients of redemptive relationship soaked in the reality of the cross—a church too often separated from its bond with the heavenly world? And as the reality of compassion doesn't shape and inform the heart I extend, then I am reduced to being a "moral, sacrificial woman" rather than a helpless child clinging to her Father, rather than a bride reflecting the radiance of a husband's pursuit and care. I am reduced to being lukewarm in my perceived spiritual wealth. As the angel said to the church in Laodicea:

You say, "I am rich. I have everything I want. I don't need a thing!" And you don't realize that you are wretched and miserable and poor and blind and naked. I advise you to buy gold from me—gold that has been purified by fire. Then you will be rich. And buy white garments so you will not be shamed by your nakedness. And buy ointment for your eyes so you will be able to see. (Revelation 3:17–18)

Compassion is allowing myself to be stunned by the absence of the bond with the heavenly world in my situation, to mourn the absence of an acknowledgment of God in my heart. It moves me to long for His presence to intrude into the most common of situations—a conversation with a friend that never gets beyond surface chatter, a relationship that has become content with maintaining a certain level of civility to avoid the deeper issues of the heart, a worship service that exalts the sacraments above the Lord of the sacraments. It is at this point that compassion and hope show their common heritage.

I hope to enjoy the splendor of Musa's heart. I hope to have the splendor of lingering with a good friend. I hope for the Bridegroom's return. And in so doing, I open my heart to compassion. To not hope is to live without compassion. To not hope is to not "go and learn what this means" (Matthew 9:13, NIV). Compassion comes whenever I'm called to ask, "The Bridegroom isn't here; where is He?"

TENDER PERSEVERANCE

Another garment of hope is tender perseverance. I don't have to tell you how long the wait can be in our alleyway of hope deferred. Charles Spurgeon once said, "By perseverance the snail reached the ark."

There's a place in the mountains where I live called the Crags. When you drive the road to the Crags before June, you will most likely find snow on the road. If you take your time, you can get to the parking area and begin your ascent on foot. At first it's not a treacherous hike—just a long, lumbering trail through a meadow of windswept grasses. Soon the trail takes on a grade up through pines and aspens, on lots of crumbling rocks. You climb and rest, climb and rest, for a while, and soon you find yourself on the top of the world, surrounded by red rock formations. It's a great place to sit, but you have to prepare yourself for the full force of the winds. It's a beautiful view, but it is not a hospitable place.

There are a handful of trees on this windswept pinnacle called bristlecone pines. If you look closely at their trunks, you see they have been twisted snarled completely in circles, shaped by the wind and ice and snow. But they have kept growing. They are some of the oldest trees on the North American continent, having been impacted by nature's force for hundreds of years. It is almost as if they grow into the face of adversity. These twisted giants are a refuge to two fluffy gray and white birds who venture out to the rock formations and sing a delightful song into the wind. Nobody knows the story the trees hold, but they are strong, and they give shelter and life in an inhospitable place.

Tender hearts give the same kind of shelter. But this comes from being shaped by the whipping gale-force winds of the alleyway. Rainer Maria Rilke recognized this in these lines:

> *You, who are almost protection where no one*
> *protects. The thought of you*
> *is like a shady sleeptree*
> *for the swarms of the solitary man.*[3]

Offering this shelter—hour by hour, hurt by hurt—is a progressive and impossible task. The apostle Paul told us,

> *Since we have been made right in God's sight by faith, we have*
> *peace with God because of what Jesus Christ our Lord has done*
> *for us. Because of our faith, Christ has brought us into this place*
> *of highest privilege where we now stand, and we confidently and*
> *joyfully look forward to sharing God's glory.*

> *We can rejoice, too, when we run into problems and trials, for we*
> *know that they are good for us—they help us learn to endure.*
> *And endurance develops strength of character in us, and character*
> *strengthens our confident expectation of salvation. And this*

expectation will not disappoint us. *For we know how dearly God loves us, because he has given us the Holy Spirit to fill our hearts with his love.* (Romans 5:1–5, emphasis added)

It can all be worth it. We can be shaped by the winds of trial with a confidence that we will give shelter and life along the way. But as C. S. Lewis said, "Probably this will not, for most of us, happen in a day; poetry replaces grammar, gospel replaces law, longing transforms obedience, as gradually as the tide lifts a grounded ship."[4]

This perseverance can be either hard or tender. We all know women who can gut it out. That's easy. Tender perseverance is an art. One of my dearest friends, Beth, knows what it is to keep on keeping on, but with passion and softness. About seven years ago, in the midst of her own struggle with depression, Beth's husband lost his job. After two years, he was finally offered a position that fully utilized his gifts and training. But then, three months later, the department was cut and so was his dream job. Most women would harden along this path. Beth has been tempted to harden. But she has learned a secret: by responding to God's love for her, she stays in a place of rest, a place only Jesus can provide. She knows this is the only way to persevere in the midst of uncertain circumstances. And she perseveres with her heart.

Responding to hope takes the edge off perseverance. It is the difference between the angry church lady who disputes the color of the new carpet for a church sanctuary, and the woman who quietly crafts an elaborate tapestry to adorn a little-known orphanage in town. It is the difference between the woman known for being a bulldog and the woman known for having chutzpah. It is the difference between concrete blocks and French doors—both are needed to build the building, but one is much more pleasing to the eye. Simone Weil says it this way: "Waiting patiently in expectation is the foundation of the spiritual life."[5] This expectation is taking us somewhere, and if we're responding to hope, the foundation can be laid with feminine, tender trust.

TENDER TRUST

So it should get easier, right? Trusting the heart of God should become more natural as time goes on? Yes and no. The good news is, the expanse of our heart cannot be measured. The perfumed scent wafting from our tears is potentially infinite. The bad news is, the more our hearts are released in beauty, the more we must trust. It is, after all, our desire—our craving for a fulfilled promise—that keeps us going. Craig Barnes says, "Imagine what would happen if God actually gave us the desire of our hearts. We would have to abandon the craving that has become so much a part of life. That would be frightening."[6] He's right. It would be terrifying. We'd be rid of that blasted ache, but we'd have very little steam to keep us going!

The author of Hebrews knew something about this. Hear his words about endurance:

> *Do not throw away this confident trust in the Lord, no matter what happens. Remember the great reward it brings you! Patient endurance is what you need now, so you will continue to do God's will. Then you will receive what he has promised.*
>
> *"For in just a little while,*
> *the Coming One will come and not delay.*
> *And a righteous person will live by faith.*
> *But I will have no pleasure in anyone who turns away."*
>
> *But we are not like those who turn their backs on God and seal their fate. We have faith that assures our salvation.* (Hebrews 10:35–39)

A FEMININE FINISH

When the bottom line becomes *who* we are waiting for, perhaps we have learned something about tender perseverance. Anna waited in the temple until the age of eighty-four just to glimpse the Messiah. Afterward, "she talked about Jesus to everyone who had been waiting for the promised King to come and deliver Jerusalem" (Luke 2:38). She knew *who* she was waiting for; I'm guessing she had no idea *how long* she'd be waiting. I certainly never knew.

Hebrews 11 is a sobering look at the kind of people who waited with faith, people who discovered the *how long* of hope. It is comforting because the people listed are so . . . well, so unfaithful. Even the "obvious faithful," including Abraham (putting Isaac on the altar) and Moses (standing up to the leader of the Egyptian empire), had glaring human frailties. But then there are others, like Rahab. She was a whore. But God saw beyond her shame to the heart that wanted to help two spies. That's beautiful. What is sobering is this:

> *All these faithful ones [those listed in Hebrews 11] died without receiving what God promised them, but they saw it all from a distance and welcomed the promises of God. They agreed that they were no more than foreigners and nomads here on earth. And obviously people who talk like that are looking forward to a country they can call their own. If they had meant the country they came from, they would have found a way to go back. But they were looking for a better place, a heavenly homeland. That is why God is not ashamed to be called their God, for he has prepared a heavenly city for them.* (Hebrews 11:13–16, emphasis added)

Can you hear what's being said here? God seems to be more concerned with our trust that we're being led somewhere, that He is taking us somewhere because of His love for us, than He is concerned with a flawless record along the way. We're also told of others who "trusted God and were tortured, preferring to die rather than turn from God and be free. They placed their hope in the resurrection to a better life" (Hebrews 11:35). They were "too good for this world" (verse 38). This is the only kind of hope that will sustain us in the dark days to come—a tenacious, scrappy, foolish, full-hearted, abandoned hope that remembers who loves us. This kind of hope keeps us tender even when the promises we've received are not fulfilled—a hope that is so centered on Jesus and where He is taking us that all else is relinquished.

BREATH OF HEAVEN

Sometimes we lose sight of who God is, let alone where He's taking us. We're heading down a path, having left our heart somewhere behind on the journey, not sure of where we're going nor of what we'll do when we get there. Again, Brent said it well, "The truth of the gospel is intended to free us to love God and others with our whole heart. When we ignore this heart aspect of our faith and try to live out our religion solely as correct doctrine or ethics, our passion is crippled, or perverted, and the divorce of our soul from the heart purposes of God toward us is deepened."[7] Tender perseverance is impossible when we live alienated from our heart.

Sometimes the only thing that rouses us from our disconnected pursuits is the breath of God. Shasta, C. S. Lewis's character from *The Horse and His Boy*, discovered this truth. He is on a road that "is bound to go somewhere," yet he's not sure at all as to his destination. Ever feel that way? Shasta is feeling quite sorry for himself. His goal is Anvard, and along the way his enemy, Rabadash, has made the trek unbearable, and his dear friend Aravis has been wounded. He has also encountered lions—many lions. Shasta doesn't know his own story or where he has left his heart. He only knows he is alone and afraid in a dark wood. It's on this road "going somewhere" through the wood that it happened. He felt the breath of the Thing (Aslan, the Christ figure) walking beside him. Shasta could not see him, but soon he found the Thing pursuing his heart as it asked Shasta to tell him his sorrows. As Shasta lamented about his journey, he was caught off guard by the response he heard.

"I do not call you unfortunate," said the Large Voice.

"Don't you think it was bad luck to meet so many lions?" said Shasta.

"There was only one lion," said the Voice.

"What on earth do you mean? I've just told you there were at least two the first night, and—"

"There was only one: but he was swift of foot."

"How do you know?"

"I was the lion. . . . I was the lion who forced you to join with Aravis. . . . I was the lion who drove the jackals from you while you slept. . . . And I was the lion you do not remember who pushed the boat in which you lay, a child near death, so that it came to shore where a man sat, wakeful at midnight, to receive you."

The Thing revealed *himself* to Shasta. He did not reveal all the answers concerning Shasta's journey. He did not reveal why he had been the one to wound his friend, Aravis. He simply revealed himself and his heart for Shasta.

It touched his forehead with its tongue. He lifted his face and their eyes met. Then instantly the pale brightness of the mist and the fiery brightness of the Lion rolled themselves together into a

swirling glory and gathered themselves up and disappeared. He
was alone with the horse on a grassy hillside under a blue sky.
And there were birds singing.[8]

Shasta's journey is where we all find ourselves when we set
out to persevere yet leave our hearts behind. Aslan's call to
Shasta is the same call Jesus breathes into our hearts: "Persevere,
but persevere *toward Me*. Let Me reveal your story to you, and
then let Me show you how it fits into Mine. Let Me show you
how much I trust your heart to finish this path, because you are
Mine."

Kathleen Norris says, "We praise God not to celebrate our
own faith but to give thanks for the faith God has in us. To let
ourselves look at God, and let God look back at us. And to
laugh, and sing, and be delighted because God has called us his
own."[9] Sometimes we have to be stunned enough by a glimpse
of Him to hear the birds of spring singing. We must be surprised by who we are, and even more surprised by the lengths
God would go to in seeking out our wandering, forgetful, foolish
hearts. Sue Monk Kidd says delight comes by way of scars.[10]
This wounded delight has the power to clear away the clouds of
doubt, allowing us to say,

Come, let us return to the LORD! *He has torn us in pieces; now*
he will heal us. He has injured us; now he will bandage our
wounds. In just a short time, he will restore us so we can live in
his presence. Oh, that we might know the LORD! *Let us press on*
to know him! Then he will respond to us as surely as the arrival
of dawn or the coming of rains in early spring. (Hosea 6:1–3)

WOUNDS AND HOPE

We so want the long journey to be one without wounds or lions
or traps. We want warmth and fulfillment, timelessness and

serenity. But hope is far more about the ecstasy of being found and led to freedom than it is about being lulled to sleep by the rhythms of God's heartbeat. If we are honest, the threshold between ecstasy and pain is slight, so it has to do more with where we are being led. Aslan had an intent for Shasta—for him to see the king with his own eyes and to know his story. Hosea had an intent for Gomer—to speak kindly to her. There are wounds, many wounds, on the way to where He is taking us. Tranquillity is the illusion; wounds can be the door of hope. His presence, often hidden, holds up our hearts and counsels us along the way, often with mere breath.

How did divine breath rouse those like Sarah, Hannah, Elizabeth, Mary, the apostle Paul, Joan of Arc, Dietrich Bonhoeffer, Aleksandr Solzhenitsyn, Mother Teresa? How does it rouse us? Sue Monk Kidd says it comes from saying yes to life in the core of our being, even when we are suffering. But what exactly are we saying yes to? We are saying yes to Him as He says, "I am taking you somewhere, and it's all about My love for you."

ENOUGH ALREADY

We'd be crazy—not human—to enter this suffering without wanting it to end. That is our hope, after all. Shasta wanted the lions to go away. We *should* anticipate suffering's end. But in the waiting we usually have our arms crossed, turning our hearts away from God with questions like "Why would God do this to me? When will He heal these wounds?"

Nicholas Wolterstorff asks a different question: "Why does God endure *his* suffering? *Why does he not at once relieve his agony by relieving ours?*"[11] (emphasis added). Do we take the time to imagine what God experiences? How can He bear to wait? Wolterstorff, whose son was killed in a rock-climbing accident, speaks to the fact that Jesus not only waits but also keeps His wounds as He waits. Wolterstorff says this—words that held up my heart following Brent's death:

"Put your hand into my wounds," said the risen Jesus to Thomas, "and you will know who I am." The wounds of Christ are his identity. They tell us who he is. He did not lose them. . . . If sympathy for the world's wounds is not enlarged by our anguish, if love for those around us is not expanded, if gratitude for what is good does not flame up, if insight is not deepened, if commitment to what is important is not strengthened, if aching for a new day is not intensified, if hope is weakened and faith diminished, if from the experience of death comes nothing good, then death has won. [12]

COURAGE AND BEAUTY

We speak of the Christian life as something that requires courage, like the courage of noble soldiers being sent to the battlefield. God gives us our marching orders, and we courageously fall into the ranks and march. Where's the tender perseverance in that? We forget that our English word *courage* comes from the French word *cœur*, which means "heart." To have courage is to have heart. We cannot be courageous in entering the world until we've been courageous in responding to God's wild love with our full heart. This is where we are either the bride of Christ or the Religious Right.

If we do not enter the internal battle for hope within our own soul, we enlist in culture wars, morality wars, theological wars, discipline wars—but our hearts are lost. As Brent said, "The waves of first love ebbed away in the whirlwind of Christian service and activity, and we began to lose the Romance. . . . We moved our spiritual life into the outer world of activity, and internally we drifted." [13] We become proficient at expressing our views on issues rather than getting to know the woman next door who has had an abortion and is needing a safe place to think through what this means for her. We become known as excellent managers of our schedules rather than as approachable and compelling women. We gain a reputation for our morality, but few have tasted our love. The internal battle takes courage. Poet David Whyte points to William Blake's definition of a mature person as "one who has entered the oceanic qualities of the soul and survived that baptism without regressing to a spontaneous but fearful second childhood."[14] This mature, courageous internal calling shapes our feminine hearts into a force to be reckoned with.

THE LOVE OF HONOR

I think of Chris, a young woman who spoke to me about her internal struggle with femininity and gender identity. She was in a treasured relationship with a woman that had taken a damaging dip into sexual gratification, and she was starting to realize that unhealthy patterns had begun months before as she was allowing this woman to depend on her, to lean on her for the kinds of strength she was not meant to provide. She genuinely wanted what was best for this woman as well as for herself.

With courage she separated from the relationship and allowed God to unearth the places inside her that were in need of His tending. She grieved that she had never really been delighted in, that she had been depended upon for strength in many inappropriate ways. Being the strong one with women was providing her a false shelter from her longings to be tender and delicate. She faced her internal war.

Chris is in no way free from her homosexual tendencies and longings. She aches with an intensity deeper than many women can comprehend. But she lives with tremendous courage. She has chosen to call herself a Christian, and she takes that mantle seriously. She desires to live a life in keeping with the convictions she holds and the tenets of the faith she has chosen. The cost for her to be a Christian is greater than we could ever conceptualize.

In knowing Chris I was reminded of God's words about Israel's stubbornness: "Their love for shame is greater than their love for honor. So a mighty wind will sweep them away. They will die in shame because they offer sacrifices to idols" (Hosea 4:18-19). It is the passions that come from the deepest place that set us free to live loving and honorable lives. The passion from the light of Christ keeps us from dying in our shame. Chris has a love for honor that holds up her heart in her unmet longings and in her confusion. Frederick Buechner speaks of that deepest place:

> *I have it in me at my best to be a saint to other people, and by saint I mean life-giver, someone who is able to bear to others something of the Holy Spirit, whom the creeds describe as the Lord and Giver of Life. Sometimes, by the grace of God, I have it in me to be Christ to other people. And so, of course, have we all — the life-giving, life-saving, and healing power to be saints . . . maybe at rare moments even to ourselves. I believe that it is when that power is alive in me and through me that I come closest to being truly home.*[5]

Again, it's what Meister Eckhart said about the birth of God's love happening in the most tender and noble place in the soul. As one woman exclaimed to me midconversation, "I never knew I had so much love in me!" When the love of honor is allowed to flow freely from the rivers of life in our hearts, when we start to glimpse a bit more of who we really are, we can't help but be in shock at how much love, passion, tenderness, and creativity live there. Now the challenge becomes actually displaying these garments of hope.

~10

SWEET REVENGE

*She'll come close enough so
you'll know she's really there.*
—BRUCE SPRINGSTEEN

*You don't have to take the whole
world on, just be tender when you want to be.*
—MARY CHAPIN CARPENTER

Ah, women.
—RAINER MARIA RILKE

Seventh grade was difficult for me. Oh, I would sit outside on springtime lunch hours with friends, we'd eat our peanut butter or yogurt with the sun on our shoulders, and all seemed right with the world. But what I wouldn't bring to those lunches or to trigonometry class was what was going on at home and what was going on in my heart. As you know, things at my home were beyond my control. Each day, dread filled my gut, and increasingly I believed I had to hold everything up, including Mom's sanity. But none of my friends were privy to this internal world.

During this time, I started to write. I would wander off to my cliff and let my mind, heart, and pen fly, taking me beyond all that was painful. It was on that cliff that I finished a creative assignment for Mrs. Schaeffer's English literature class. I wrote an "epic" poem about a young boy and girl who wandered, hand in hand, through coves on a beach. With every cove they entered, with each adventure and mystery, their care and delight in one another became more obvious. Two young lives caught up in friendship and love.

The day came for us to present our creative work to Mrs. Schaeffer and the class. I was called on to present my work, and I felt the predictable junior-high nerves. But as I began to read, I was caught up in the wonder of each cove, each cave, each spray of ocean mist, each kind glance between these two. I was taken away to a place where love opened up a whole new world. As I read the last few lines, I was slowly brought back to Mrs. Schaeffer's class. With embarrassment, I looked up at my classmates, only to see looks of utter disbelief on their faces. Absolute silence. For a moment I wondered if I had made a grand fool of myself. After many long moments of silence, a boy in the second row who I didn't know well said, "There is *no way* you wrote that." A few other kids around him started to nod in agreement, but then looked at me as if to say, *"Did* you?" I was shocked. I didn't know how to respond. Mrs. Schaeffer made her way to the front of the class, put her hand on my shoulder, and said, "I can guarantee you she wrote that herself. It is a work of art, Jan."

What a collision! The sheer joy of Mrs. Schaeffer's words collided with the shame that flooded my soul. I wanted to run. The look on my classmates' faces said to me, "That's too much—it is too lovely. It is far too good to be from you! If you create from your heart, give of your internal world, then suddenly you are not one of us anymore." Jean-Paul Sartre said that shame is a hemorrhage of the soul—I found out what that meant. Hope was finding me, and I was welcoming it, as I wrote that poem. In Mrs. Schaeffer's class I came to realize that the substance of hope is not always welcomed.

Wearing Our Loveliness

Why is the substance of hope not always welcomed? Don't we want everyone to be as lovely, as vibrant, as creative, as beautiful as they can be? We think we do, but we really don't.

Several years ago there were news reports about the Sistene Chapel. Evidently, the Italian proprietors of this exquisite historical and spiritual treasure decided to test a new process for cleaning antiquities. They were overwhelmed by the color, the vibrancy, the detail that emerged in the cleaning. Beauty that had been hidden under centuries of grime, street dirt, and moisture was revealed. Fastidiously, the chapel was transformed from one end to the other, a process that took several years. As the mire was cleared away, the creation was suddenly so much more lifelike, so much more human. Michelangelo's intention was once again revealed to those who had known only a marred substitute.

The artistic community was pleased. The common folk, however, went into an uproar. Citizens who had come to know the chapel dulled by grime demanded vigorously to "have their painting back!" There was little sense that the true treasure had been unveiled. "The new painting is too much!" they cried. There was only outrage that the marred image was gone.

Amazing, isn't it? When we get a glimpse of what was intended, it makes us remember. We don't want to remember. Looking from the alleyway back into the restaurant, smelling the fine meal, asks something of us. Glory asks something of us. Our hearts say, "Leave us alone; we're fine. Please don't unveil our faces, because we're not sure how the glory will be handled." It might be too much. We would rather have the comfort of a marred painting than deal with the brilliance of the original. The beauty of revealed hope is often met with such disdain.

THE BEAUTY OF HOPE

We all give in to the temptation to tone down our beauty, so it amazes me when hearts responsive to hope show up, unveiling feminine masterpieces. Certain women come to mind, women who are not just dutifully giving of themselves. Rather, they are—in the middle of the alleyways and ache of their lives— choosing to love. Their imagination runs toward others. Gerald May says, "Evil is irrevocably at cross-purposes with love, life, freedom and creation. . . . Evil continues to work against God, but with no chance of ultimate success."[1] That's what these women tell me with their lives—evil has tried hard to have their hearts, but it is losing. Their lives send laughter through the kingdom. It is the laughter of Isaiah 14:16-17 as we ask, "Is *this* the one whom we feared?"

I think of Pat, who after thirty years of marriage found her hope for retirement—enjoying grandchildren and growing old with the man she loved—dashed as her husband chose to have an affair with a much younger woman in his office. It took courage for her to face some of the ways she had disconnected herself from good involvement with him through the years (when we met, she was the classic church lady). But Pat went further and kept her heart open and hopeful as she watched her husband's heart grow hardened toward her, Christianity, and all they had held dear. She grieved as he determined to marry this younger woman.

Watching Pat's journey was silencing because she allowed God's vision of her heart to grow (the church lady exchanged that image for one of being a fiery mare who was ready to run wild through the countryside). As she did this, she was more passionate and lovely than ever. And she was more lonely—she was now aware of just how much she had to give. I marveled as I watched this woman tenderly pray for her former husband and his new marriage.

I think of a friend who has known untold horror. From a

rural backwoods community, she was the only one in her family to graduate from high school, let alone finish graduate school, which she did with flying colors. She's known horrific sexual abuse from family members, neighbors, and strangers, all because there was complete disregard for her heart in the context of her family. Today she is a vibrant woman. She struggles with periods of darkness but lives life with the allure of hope. An interaction with her sounds like this:

ME: "What are you hoping for?"

MY FRIEND: "I've been hoping to live as fully as possible my whole life; I keep fighting to live, and hope often fades, obscured by despair. Each time it is more painful to regain the hope."

ME: "So, why do you?"

MY FRIEND: "There is no alternative but death."

ME: "Why not choose that?"

MY FRIEND: "As hard as I've tried, I can't kill my heart. God has hold of it, and I can't force Him to let go. I've tried, but the more I'm sought out by His love, the more free I am. As much as hope relieves the despair, it also really does make the heart sick—when I'm disappointed, when hope isn't realized in the timing I want. If I'm going to be alive and have hope, I'm going to have to grieve my losses and risk being hurt again and again.

"Because of the way God has a hold on me, I can't stop myself from putting my whole heart into life. A good part of the time this brings happiness, joy, and peace, but it also opens me up to deeper levels of despair. I've known abandonment, rejection, abuse, insane countless tragedies and horrors. Apart from God, there is no reason I should be here, that I'd ever want to choose life. But what He's given me—His love—it makes me unable to resist giving these things away to other people."

ME: "What fuels you to keep going?"

MY FRIEND: "A desire to leave a mark, a better legacy than

the one I was given. To give birth to life—to give so children can flourish and not fight to survive. As long as I don't know the reality of actual childbirth, I will love other people's children, give my heart away to them, my friends. I want to impact them and change their lives."

MUSTERED HOPE

Contrast the above conversation with one I had with a single mother, Rebecca, who works hard at an airport restaurant to support herself and her three girls. It became clear to me, in talking to Rebecca, that she, too, wants to leave her mark, wants to give life. Of course she does—she is a woman made in the image of God. But Rebecca floundered when talking about hope. Though she tried to come up with a hope that would convince her of her own internal strength, she didn't do well at it. This is what the labored conversation with her sounded like:

ME: "What keeps you going day to day?"

REBECCA: "I had a difficult childhood. I had an alcoholic father and five siblings, and I never knew whether we would be cared for. I craved stability. And I crave stability now, especially for my kids. Predictably, I married an alcoholic. He was younger than me. I've kept things focused on the kids. They all have had straight As and have been on the honor roll.

"I always have lived thinking, *Let me know when the bad will hit me.* I've had an abortion. I've been stalked. I guess I hope for others. I can't change things for them, but I can hope for them."

ME: "How do you hope for yourself?"

REBECCA: "I guess I punch in a positive attitude."

ME: "Does it work?"

REBECCA: "It does for a while, but I'm still alone. I guess it is better to be alone than in bad company. I guess I hope to get rid of the bad. I hope for someone to appreciate who I am."

Deflates us to listen to this, doesn't it? But listen carefully. As strained as Rebecca's responses are, they are responses that are often applauded as Christian. Rebecca is cheerleading her own heart, holding herself up with mustered perspective. She has to. Rebecca has not yet come to understand the love that Christ has for her. She has nothing else until she comes to understand who Jesus is. But how often do you and I "punch in" a positive attitude and put a stamp of Christ's approval on it? In doing so, we never need to be found outside the Restaurant—we're getting along just fine. We have no need of a Savior.

These women have been thrust into the alleyway, but the encounters with them are so different. We walk away from the conversation with my friend strengthened and thirsty. She is desperate to be found in the alleyway and isn't ashamed of that. Sharon Hersh says,

> When a woman courageously stares into the eyes of her desperation, she need not collapse in shame or cover up with pretense. The yearning for relationship is not an indication that something is wrong with her, but that something is profoundly right. When the desperation of God is appropriated to our own desperate hearts, a breakthrough into extravagantly loving others occurs.[2]

We walk away from my conversation with Rebecca aching for her to know that hope isn't up to her. She is so much more than a punched-in positive attitude. So are we all.

WEARING LOVE

The loneliness of the alleyway is a great place to sit at one another's feet, to inquire of others out there, "What's this like for you? I'm not liking it much; how about you? How are we going to make it? Where do you think Jesus is? Do you remember what He told us? Do you believe it?" Macrina Wiederkehr says that if you've found someone who has lived fully and is still fully alive, you've found a treasure—learn from her.[3] Being fully alive for others in the alleyway is being who Jesus was for us: a servant. And the most radiant service flows from our deepest place of need. Second Corinthians says that our hope—this precious treasure, this light and power that now shine within us—is held in perishable containers, that is, in our weak bodies. So everyone can see that our glorious power is from God and is not our own (2 Corinthians 4:7).

When a woman's heart rests in the truth that the only thing left in the alleyway is to love others, then she lives from the allure of hope. And this comes only after a deep acknowledgment that God must find her, must love her in spite of herself. Henri Nouwen says, "The true voice of love is a very soft and gentle voice speaking to me in the most hidden places of my being. It is not a boisterous voice, forcing itself on me and demanding attention. It is the voice of a nearly blind father who has cried much and died many deaths. It is a voice that can only be heard by those who allow themselves to be touched."[4]

It is a quiet reminder of God's eyes toward us that draws us away from contemptuous hovering and the bitter retribution of clamoring. Only in remembering the voice that calls us "beloved" can we extend our hearts to those who have harmed us, or stay alive in circumstances beyond our control. What does that mean? It means Jesus calls us to give of our hearts in ways we can't. He calls us to forgive those who have hurt us—something we can't do on our own.

This quiet reminder calls us to admit our need to be touched, to be forgiven for wandering away from His love. Dan Allender says, "We continue to play with the gospel rather than allowing the gospel to play with us."[5] As we allow ourselves to rest, to gaze back through the restaurant window and remember the kind eyes of the chef who prepared the too-good-to-be-true meal, as we allow ourselves to envision the day when the meal will be restored in fullness, then we remember our need to be found, to be touched, to be forgiven. Then the gospel has played with us. The allure of hope gives birth to a simple, sacred plea. This plea was spoken by a Russian peasant in *The Way of a Pilgrim:* "Have mercy on me, a sinner, O Lord Jesus Christ."[6]

During the long wait, God rouses our desire, keeping us persevering in an alleyway that will be swallowed up in one resounding, trumpeted moment of beauty. We'll discover then what it is like to have the Father run down the road toward our prodigal hearts, exuberant over the feast about to begin in our honor. And it will be lavish. We'll begin the true process of knowing the Savior we've only been introduced to on earth. We'll see. We'll drink. We'll smell. We'll dance. We'll look at each other with a sense of "Oh, so *that's* who you are!" We'll receive the identity only Jesus has known was there all along.

Our desire in the long wait reminds us of who we're waiting for. He is taking us somewhere, and along the way He is creating beauty. Our responsive, sensual, compassionate, forgiving, persevering hearts have the privilege of introducing others to this Glorious Intruder, this Chef who creates elaborately with us in mind, this One who seeks us out amid our hovering and clamoring false pursuits of femininity.

BEAUTY'S MYSTERY

There is a mystery to the beauty we offer as women—it has an alluring power unlike any other because it is offered in alleyways and distress. It is seen most in those who are not trying to be beautiful but are simply being women. Maria Rilke captures this:

Ah, women, that you are here on earth, that you
move here among us, grief-filled,
no more watched over than we and yet able
to bless like the blessed.

From what region,
when the loved one appears,
do you take the future?

More than will ever exist.
He who knows distances
up to the outermost fixed star
is amazed to find this,
your magnificent heartspace.
How, in the crush, do you keep it free?[7]

Yes. That's just it. How do we keep the spaciousness of our heart free? The allure of hope is that our hearts are *set* free. We can acknowledge our hovering and clamoring, open our hearts to vision, allow ourselves to be caught in our addictions. But it is only when a woman is broken over her mistrust of God's heart, when she allows herself to weep over the ways she maneuvers for control, when she owns her harm of others, that she can look into the stunning reality of His merciful eyes. And His eyes call us home — home to freedom.

Such a woman is mysteriously beautiful. Her deep confidence that her heart will be found allows her to explore and examine philosophies, religions, cultures, the dark places of her own heart, and other people with freedom and confidence. Those around her are compelled to wonder because she is beyond anything they've ever seen.

CARRIED AWAY

In the mountains, a few days shortly after Brent died, I fell asleep beside the Chalk Creek, which was running high. I woke up with a start when I heard a noise, and I looked up to find a baby deer caught in the current at the far side of the river. I sat up, screaming, because she was being knocked against the rocks. I could not get to her, so in my helplessness I pleaded, "Please, God. Save her." She was carried a bit farther and then landed on a sandbar.

She slowly got up on her spindly, feeble legs, and then she turned around and looked directly at me, as if to ask, "What do

I do now?" I had no idea how far upstream her mother was, had no way of knowing whether she would survive. She wandered off into the brush, and I had to surrender her to the kind hand of God.

It wasn't until much later that I realized God had given me this little deer to show me exactly how I was. I was not okay. God said, "Something has come and carried you away, and you have been knocked and bruised. I see you. I'll take care of you."

Many months later I returned to the river with a dear friend. As we pulled into the same spot, my friend—who knew the story—whispered, "Jan, look." Across the river, on the same sandbar, stood a young female deer, barely losing her spots. She stood alone, looking at me. My friend wept and said, "I think she's going to be okay."

We've heard You, Jesus. You've awakened us. We're alive. Your current is taking us somewhere beyond telling. Breathe on us. Find us. Save us. Soon.

Notes

CHAPTER ONE — THE ACHE THAT DOESN'T GO AWAY

1. Antoine de Saint-Exupéry, *The Little Prince,* trans. Katherine Woods (San Diego: Harcourt Brace Jovanovich, 1993), p. 87.
2. Gerald G. May, *Addiction and Grace* (San Francisco: Harper & Row, 1988), p. 179.
3. Quoted in Jim Arnholtz, ed., *New Mexico on My Mind* (Helena, Mont.: Falcon, 1990), p. 16.
4. Brent Curtis and John Eldredge, *The Sacred Romance: Drawing Closer to the Heart of God* (Nashville: Nelson, 1997), p. 23.

CHAPTER TWO — THE PATH OF HOVERING

1. Gerald G. May, *Addiction and Grace* (San Francisco: Harper & Row, 1988), p. 93.
2. Frederick Buechner, *A Room Called Remember: Uncollected Pieces* (San Francisco: Harper & Row, 1984), pp. 1-5.
3. Ruth Bell Graham, untitled poem in *Sitting by My Laughing Fire* (Waco, Tex.: Word, 1977), p. 64.
4. Ayn Rand, *The Fountainhead* (Indianapolis: Bobbs-Merrill, 1968), p. 180.
5. Brent Curtis and John Eldredge, *The Sacred Romance: Drawing Closer to the Heart of God* (Nashville: Nelson, 1997), p. 108.
6. Karen Lee-Thorpe and Cynthia Hicks, *Why Beauty Matters* (Colorado Springs, Colo.: NavPress, 1997), p. 95.

CHAPTER THREE — THE PATH OF CLAMORING

1. George Gordon Lord Byron, "She Walks in Beauty," quoted in John Miller, ed., *Beauty: An Anthology by John Miller* (San Francisco: Chronicle, 1997), p. 238.
2. Helen Gurley Brown, "The Late Show" in *Beauty,* p. 186.
3. Brown, "Late Show," p. 187.
4. Brown, "Late Show," p. 169.
5. Sharon Hersh, "The Desperation of God: A Reflection on the Feminine Desire for Relationship," *Mars Hill Review* 9 (Fall 1997): 19-29.
6. Naomi Wolf, "The Beauty Myth" in *Beauty,* p. 266.
7. Karen Lee-Thorpe and Cynthia Hicks, *Why Beauty Matters* (Colorado Springs, Colo.: NavPress, 1997), p. 95.

CHAPTER FOUR—THE FOOLISH PATH OF HOPE

1. Frederick Buechner, *The Longing for Home: Recollections and Reflections* (San Francisco: HarperSanFrancisco, 1996), p. 109.
2. Buechner, *Longing for Home*, p. 110.
3. M. Craig Barnes, *When God Interrupts: Finding New Life Through Unwanted Change* (Downers Grove, Ill.: InterVarsity, 1996), p. 39.
4. Macrina Wiederkehr, *A Tree Full of Angels: Seeing the Holy in the Ordinary* (San Francisco: Harper & Row, 1988), p. 90.
5. C. S. Lewis, *The Weight of Glory and Other Addresses* (New York: Touchstone, 1975), p. 37.
6. John Powell, *The Christian Vision: The Truth That Sets Us Free* (Allen, Tex.: Argus, 1984), p. 29.
7. Dallas Willard, *The Spirit of the Disciplines: Understanding How God Changes Lives* (San Francisco: Harper & Row, 1988), p. 227.
8. Buechner, *Longing for Home*, p. 110.
9. Lewis, *Weight of Glory*, p. 37.
10. Kathleen Norris, *Amazing Grace: A Vocabulary of Faith* (New York: Riverhead, 1998), p. 211.
11. Lewis, *Weight of Glory*, p. 38.
12. Dan B. Allender, *The Cry of the Soul: How Our Emotions Reveal Our Deepest Questions About God* (Colorado Springs, Colo.: NavPress, 1994), p. 23.
13. Allender, *Cry of the Soul*, p. 23.
14. Fyodor Dostoyevsky, *The Brothers Karamazov*, trans. Richard Pevear and Larissa Volokhonsky (New York: Knopf, 1992), p. 320.
15. Thomas Merton, *No Man Is an Island* (London: Harvest/Harcourt Brace Jovanovich, 1983), p. 202.
16. Frederick Buechner, *Godric* (San Francisco: HarperSanFrancisco, 1988), p. 7.
17. Peterson speaks often of this throughout his *Under the Predictable Plant: An Exploration in Vocational Holiness* (Grand Rapids, Mich.: Eerdmans, 1992).
18. Buechner, *Longing for Home*, p. 26.

CHAPTER FIVE—BOREDOM AND BREAD

1. C. S. Lewis, *The Weight of Glory and Other Addresses* (New York: Touchstone, 1975), p. 27.
2. Dan B. Allender, "Facing Evil as a Crime Victim," *Mars Hill Review* 11 (Summer 1998): 35.
3. Oswald Chambers, *My Utmost for His Highest* (New York: Dodd, Mead, 1935), August 5.
4. Robin Norwood, *Women Who Love Too Much: When You Keep Wishing and Hoping He'll Change* (New York: Pocket Books, 1986), p. 40.

5. Norwood, *Women Who Love Too Much*, p. 36.

6. Judson Cornwall, *Let Us Draw Near* (Plainfield, N.J.: Logos, 1977), p. 145.

CHAPTER SIX—DAILY DESIRE

1. Meister Eckhart, "Sermon 21: Three Births: Ours, God's and Ourselves and God's Children," quoted in Matthew Fox, *Breakthrough: Meister Eckhart's Creation Spirituality* (New York: Image/Doubleday, 1981), p. 290.

2. Sue Monk Kidd, *When the Heart Waits: Spiritual Direction for Life's Sacred Questions* (San Francisco: Harper & Row, 1990), p. 148.

3. Kidd, *When the Heart Waits*, p. 148.

4. Gerald G. May, *Addiction and Grace* (San Francisco: Harper & Row, 1988), p. 91.

5. Hudson speaks of this in his seminar "Romancing the Heart." Information is available through Mars Hill Forum, 321 High School Rd. NE 384, Bainbridge Island, WA 98111.

6. Rodney Clapp, *Families at the Crossroads: Beyond Traditional and Modern Options* (Downers Grove, Ill.: InterVarsity, 1993).

7. Kidd, *When the Heart Waits*, p. 200.

8. M. Craig Barnes, *When God Interrupts: Finding New Life Through Unwanted Change* (Downers Grove, Ill.: InterVarsity, 1996), p. 54.

9. Kathleen Norris, *Amazing Grace: A Vocabulary of Faith* (New York: Riverhead, 1998), p. 273.

10. May, *Addiction and Grace*, p. 118.

11. May, *Addiction and Grace*, p. 135.

12. Henri J. M. Nouwen, *The Path of Waiting* (New York: Crossroad, 1995), p. 26.

CHAPTER SEVEN—YEARNING FOR HEAVEN

1. A. W. Tozer, *The Divine Conquest* (New York: Revell, 1950), p. 101.

2. C. S. Lewis, *The Weight of Glory and Other Addresses* (New York: Touchstone, 1975), p. 28.

3. Lewis, *Weight of Glory*, p. 28.

4. Quoted in Kathleen Norris, *Amazing Grace: A Vocabulary of Faith* (New York: Riverhead, 1998), p. 368.

5. Norris, *Amazing Grace*, p. 368.

6. Blaise Pascal, "Seeking the Wrong Thing," quoted in Paul Oftstedal, ed., *Daily Readings from Spiritual Classics* (Minneapolis: Augsburg, 1990), p. 141.

7. Kelly Monroe, "Our Hope on the Journey," quoted in Christopher de Vinck, *Nouwen Then: Personal Reflections on Henri* (Grand Rapids, Mich.: Zondervan, 1999), p. 101.

8. Gerald G. May, *Addiction and Grace* (San Francisco: Harper & Row, 1988), p. 96.

9. Philip Yancey, *Disappointment with God: Three Questions No One Asks Aloud* (New York: HarperCollins, 1985), p. 126.

10. Robert Bly, *Iron John: A Book About Men* (New York: Vintage, 1992), p. 86.

11. Peter Kreeft, *Making Sense out of Suffering* (Ann Arbor, Mich.: Servant, 1986), p. 153.

12. Sheldon Vanauken, *A Severe Mercy* (New York: Harper & Row, 1979), p. 125.

13. Lewis, *Weight of Glory,* p. 29

14. George MacDonald, "To Lily, 1891," quoted in Rolland Hein, ed., *The Heart of George MacDonald: A One-Volume Collection of His Most Important Fiction, Essays, Sermons, Drama, Poetry, Letters* (Wheaton, Ill: Harold Shaw, 1994), p. 15.

15. Sharon Hersh, "The Desperation of God: A Reflection on the Feminine Desire for Relationship," *Mars Hill Review* 9 (Fall 1997): 19-29.

16. Lewis, *Weight of Glory,* p. 30.

17. M. Scott Peck, "Battling Sexual Indiscretion," *Ministry* (January 1987): 4-6.

18. T. S. Eliot, "Little Gidding" from "Four Quartets" in *Collected Poems, 1909–1962* (London: Faber, 1974).

19. MacDonald, "To Adelaide Pym, 1890," in *Heart of George MacDonald,* p. 14.

20. John Piper, *Desiring God: Meditations of a Christian Hedonist* (Sisters, Oreg.: Multnomah, 1986), p. 69.

21. Kreeft, *Making Sense,* p. 98.

22. MacDonald, "To Adelaide Pym," p. 13.

23. Nicholas Wolterstorff, *Lament for a Son* (Grand Rapids, Mich.: Eerdmans, 1987), p. 67.

24. MacDonald, "To Adelaide Pym," p. 14.

CHAPTER EIGHT — OUR LOVER'S EYES

1. Kathleen Norris, *Amazing Grace: A Vocabulary of Faith* (New York: Riverhead, 1998), p. 151.

2. Sharon Hersh, "The Desperation of God: A Reflection on the Feminine Desire for Relationship," *Mars Hill Review* 9 (Fall 1997): 19-29.

3. Albert Schweitzer, *The Quest of the Historical Jesus: A Critical Study of Its Progress from Reimarus to Wrede* (London: Black, 1936), p. 401.

4. Johannes Tauler, "Thirst for God," quoted in *Daily Readings from Spiritual Classics,* ed. Paul Ofstedal (Minneapolis: Augsburg, 1990), p. 285.

5. Simone Weil, "Waiting," quoted in *Daily Readings from Spiritual Classics,* p. 347.

6. David Hazard, ed., *Early Will I Seek You: A Forty-Day Journey in the Company of Augustine* (Minneapolis: Bethany, 1991), p. 82.

7. M. Craig Barnes, *When God Interrupts: Finding New Life Through Unwanted Change* (Downers Grove, Ill.: InterVarsity, 1996), p. 39.

8. Hazard, *Early Will I Seek You,* p. 83.
9. Macrina Wiederkehr, *A Tree Full of Angels: Seeing the Holy in the Ordinary* (San Francisco: Harper & Row, 1988), p. 26.
10. Norris, *Amazing Grace,* p. 151.

CHAPTER NINE — HOPE'S ATTIRE

1. David Henderson, "Rounding the Cape of Good Hope," *Discipleship Journal,* (Fall 1999), p. 5.
2. Fyodor Dostoyevsky, *The Brothers Karamazov,* trans. Richard Pevear and Larissa Volokhonsky (New York: Knopf, 1992), p. 245.
3. Rainer Maria Rilke, "Antistrophes" in *Uncollected Poems,* trans. Edward Snow (New York: North Point, 1996), p. 143.
4. C. S. Lewis, *The Weight of Glory and Other Addresses* (New York: Touchstone, 1975), p. 27.
5. Quoted in Sue Monk Kidd, *When the Heart Waits: Spiritual Direction for Life's Sacred Questions* (San Francisco: Harper & Row, 1990), p. 21.
6. M. Craig Barnes, *When God Interrupts: Finding New Life Through Unwanted Change* (Downers Grove, Ill.: InterVarsity, 1996), p. 38.
7. Brent Curtis and John Eldredge, *The Sacred Romance: Drawing Closer to the Heart of God* (Nashville: Nelson, 1997), p. 9.
8. C. S. Lewis, *The Horse and His Boy* (New York: HarperCollins, 1994), pp. 155-160.
9. Kathleen Norris, *Amazing Grace: A Vocabulary of Faith* (New York: Riverhead, 1998), p. 151.
10. Kidd, *When the Heart Waits,* p. 184.
11. Nicholas Wolterstorff, *Lament for a Son* (Grand Rapids, Mich.: Eerdmans, 1987), p. 90.
12. Wolterstorff, *Lament,* p. 92.
13. Curtis and Eldredge, *Sacred Romance,* p. 7.
14. David Whyte, *The Heart Aroused: Poetry and the Preservation of the Soul in Corporate America* (New York: Currency Doubleday, 1994), p. 29.
15. Frederick Buechner, *The Longing for Home: Recollections and Reflections* (San Francisco: HarperSanFrancisco, 1996), p. 28.

CHAPTER TEN — SWEET REVENGE

1. Gerald G. May, *Addiction and Grace* (San Francisco: Harper & Row, 1988), p. 118.
2. Sharon Hersh, "The Desperation of God: A Reflection on the Feminine Desire for Relationship," *Mars Hill Review* 9 (Fall 1997): 19-29.
3. Macrina Wiederkehr, *A Tree Full of Angels: Seeing the Holy in the Ordinary* (San Francisco: Harper & Row, 1988), p. 35.

4. Henri J. M. Nouwen, *The Return of the Prodigal Son: A Story of Homecoming* (New York: Image, 1994), p. 40.
5. Dan B. Allender, "Bold Love", seminar presented at Pathways Church, Denver, Colo., April 2000.
6. Helen Bacovcin, trans, *The Way of a Pilgrim and The Pilgrim Continues His Way: A New Translation*, (New York: Image/Doubleday, 1978), pp. 121-123.
7. Rainer Maria Rilke, "Antistrophes" in *Uncollected Poems*, trans. Edward Snow (New York: North Point, 1996), p. 143.

WEIPPE PUBLIC LIBRARY
P. O. Box 435
Street E.
Weippe, Idaho 83553

About the Author

Jan Meyers received her B.A. in psychology from Biola University and her M.A. in counseling from Colorado Christian University. Jan was a missionary with O. C. International in Southern Africa from 1988 to 1991. She did her professional internship under the supervision of Dr. Larry Crabb and Dr. Dan Allender, and has been a licensed professional counselor in Colorado since 1994.

Jan has conducted "The Allure of Hope" women's seminars in the United States and overseas, and she has served as a guest speaker for The Sacred Romance lecture series. Jan has been a counselor for Wounded Heart Recovery Weeks with Dr. Dan Allender. Her work has been published in The *Mars Hill Review*.

After working as counselor in private practice in Colorado Springs for eight years, Jan will be relocating to Charlotte, North Carolina, to join The Barnabas Center, an ecumenical counseling, training, and writing ministry. Moving to the South will be quite a challenge for a western girl who doesn't like cheese grits. Jan loves to cook, ski, and hike. She also loves her dog.

The *Allure of Hope* has been a several-year project that has tested Jan's own understanding of hope. During the writing of this book, Jan lost one of her best friends (counselor Brent Curtis), had a broken engagement, and saw her hometown of Los Alamos, New Mexico, burn. The *Allure of Hope* is her first book.

WEIPPE PUBLIC LIBRARY
P. O. Box 435
105 N. 1st Street E.
Weippe, Idaho 83553

YOUR FEAR AND ANXIETY CAN FURTHER YOUR FAITH.

Tame Your Fears

In *Tame Your Fears*, Carol Kent examines ten fears common to
most women. Discover how to overcome such fears—disappointing
people, being rejected, getting trapped—by using them
as stepping stones to deeper faith, renewed confidence, and
sincere reverence for a powerful and loving God.
Tame Your Fears (Carol Kent) $13

Calm My Anxious Heart

If you're tired of worrying about all the "what-ifs" in your life
and want to experience the calm and contentment promised in
Scripture, *Calm My Anxious Heart* is for you! Filled with
encouragement and practical help for overcoming anxiety,
this book includes a twelve-week Bible study.
Calm My Anxious Heart (Linda Dillow) $14

Get your copies today at your local bookstore, visit our website at
www.navpress.com, or call (800) 366-7788 and ask for offer
#6136 or a FREE catalog of NavPress products.

NAVPRESS
BRINGING TRUTH TO LIFE
www.navpress.com

Prices subject to change.